D0051869

New Chicana/Chicano Writing

NEW CHICANA/ CHICANO WRITING

1

Charles M. Tatum, Editor

THE UNIVERSITY OF ARIZONA PRESS
Tucson & London

About the Editor

CHARLES M. TATUM is professor of Spanish and head of the
Department of Spanish and Portuguese at the University of
Arizona, where he also teaches Chicano and Latin American
literature. He has published extensively in the areas of
Chicano literature, Latin American literature, and Latin
American popular culture. He is the author of *Chicano
Literature*, translated and published in Spanish in 1986.
Tatum was also for several years editor of publications of the
Latin American Literary Review. He is coeditor of the
journal *Studies in Latin American Popular Culture*.

The University of Arizona Press
Copyright © 1992
The Arizona Board of Regents
All Rights Reserved

♾ This book is printed on acid-free, archival-quality paper.
Manufactured in the United States of America.

97 96 95 94 6 5 4 3

New Chicana/Chicano writing
ISSN 1058-2770

Contents

Introduction	xi
ALICIA GASPAR DE ALBA	
Juana Inés	1
JOEL HUERTA	
Largesse	16
Splendid Duty	17
South Texas Minimal	18
Lowrider Car	19
WalMart America Quartet	20
Humdrum Pageants	20
Ozzy	21
Honda Automotive, a Dream	21
WalMart Discount City	22
Gulf of Mexico, Fireworks	23
Some Angel, or Winged Star	24
The Beauty Nook Hair Salon, 1965	25
ODILIA GALVÁN RODRÍGUEZ	
Mud Boy	27
Muralist	29
Sequoia Sempervirens	30
Migratory Birds	31
LUIS OMAR SALINAS	
Barefoot with a Rose	35
To Our Amigos	35
Night Waltz	37
Pieces	38

GLORIA ANZALDÚA

Ghost Trap	40
Puddles	43

ELBA SÁNCHEZ

Los desterrados/Uprooted	46
Pueblo pintor/Living Canvas	47
Espejismo: Mujer poesía/Mirror Image: Womanpoetry	48

BERNICE ZAMORA

Tere	51

GARY SOTO

Home Course in Religion	56
A Sunday	59
Drinking in the Sixties	65

ALFRED ARTEAGA

Canto 12: Letters of Color	67

ANDRÉS RODRÍGUEZ

Banners	70
Fire and Water	73
To My Mother	74

SANDRA CISNEROS

Divine Providence	76

RAY GONZÁLEZ

The Energy of Clay	79
The Blue Snake	83
Homage to Lucian Blaga	84

FRANCISCO X. ALARCÓN

Lamentario/Lamentary	89
Pobres poetas/Poor Poets	90
Silence	90
We Are Trees	91
Isla Mujeres	92
Extranjero/Foreigner	92

IVÁN ARGÜELLES
These Things   93
Curriculum Vitae   94
ENRIQUE BERUMEN
Corner   97
Nelson   97
NORMA CANTÚ
Se me enchina el cuerpo al oír tu cuento . . . 101
C. S. FOSTER
No Matches   103
Mr. & Mrs. McCluskey   104
RAMÓN GARCÍA
La piñata: A Self-portrait   106
For Frida Kahlo   106
PAT MORA
The Young Sor Juana   108
HELENA MARÍA VIRAMONTES
Tears on My Pillow   110
CÉSAR A. GONZÁLEZ-T.
Los Scholarships I   116
Los Scholarships II   117
JUAN FELIPE HERRERA
Blowfish: An Autobiography   119
VICTORIANO MARTÍNEZ
Shoes   142
Along the River   143
There's No Stopping   143
Rain   144
Alphabet   145
BARBARA RENAUD GONZÁLEZ
The Summer of Vietnam   147

MARIE-ELISE WHEATWIND
Los Perdidos: "Catalina"   149
DARREN J. DE LEÓN
Extra Innings   151
Lawless Prose   152
RAÚL NIÑO
February on Eighteenth Street   154
ORLANDO RAMÍREZ
The Awakening   158
For Your Fellow Man   161
Enough That   162
Affection   163
Meetings with a Saint   165
Translating   166
The Road of Life   166
Jewel Lake   167
On the Way of Vegas   168
Soup   169
In Kensington   170
DOROTEA REYNA
My Father   171
Voice   172
JOEL ANTONIO VILLALÓN
Blue Day   175
About the Contributors   179

"My hands are strong and from within I rule."
Pat Mora

Introduction

Charles M. Tatum

There are some striking similarities between the state of
African-American literature forty years ago and the state
today of Chicano literature. In the case of the former, literature by African-American writers experienced phenomenal
growth in the 1940s and the 1950s, yet mainstream publishers,
public schools and universities, trade magazines, professional
journals and associations, and most scholars and teachers of
American literature refused to acknowledge its intrinsic value
and contribution to the canon of American letters. Much of
this resistance gave way in the 1960s due in large measure to
the legitimate demands of civil rights groups and African-
American leaders to bring down the walls of discrimination,
racism, and exclusion.

Once African-American literature was admitted into the
classroom, placed on reading lists, and accepted and published
by mainstream publishers and academic presses, only the
most intransigent teachers and scholars refused to recognize
its legitimate place in American literature. While pockets of
resistance still exist today, few would dispute the value of
African-American literature's aesthetics, literary worth,
trenchant social commentary, and exploration of an essential
dimension of the American experience.

Like African-American literature four decades back, Chicano literature during the past decade has enjoyed a period of
unprecedented growth and vigor and will soon share, if it
does not already, the same legitimate place in the American
social, cultural, and literary mainstream. Among the several
indicators of its health are the number and prestige of trade,
university, and small presses who are publishing works by
Chicano authors. Houghton Mifflin, Knopf, Random House,
Harcourt Brace Jovanovich, William Morrow, New Directions,

and Chronicle Books are a few of the commercial houses that have recently published a wide range of this minority literature or that have contracted with promising writers for their works. A few university presses that already have published (or soon will publish) both creative literature and critical studies on Chicano literature are the University of Texas Press, the University of California Press, the University of Pittsburgh Press, the University of New Mexico Press, Duke University Press, and the University of Wisconsin Press. Small presses with an ambitious combined publications program of more than one hundred titles are Arte Público Press and Bilingual Press. Other small presses with significant Chicano literature publications are West End Press, Beacon Press, Cibola Press, Alexandrian Press, Sheep Meadow Press, Confluence Press, and Strawberry Hill Press.

Another indication of growth and recognition can be seen in the increasing popularity of Spanish-language Chicano literature published in Mexico. University of Arizona professor Miguel Méndez, for example, has recently signed contracts with important Mexican publishers, Posada and Era, to republish *Peregrinos de Aztlán* and *El sueño de Santa María de las Piedras*, and to publish other works of prose and poetry for the first time. Their wide network of distribution will place Méndez's works throughout the Spanish-speaking world. A recent review appearing in the Mexico City cultural supplement, *Siempre*, hailed *Peregrinos de Aztlán* as one of the most important Mexican novels of this century. Other writers who have recently published in Mexico are Ricardo Aguilar and Sergio Elizondo.

Another measure of the excellent quality of Chicano writing is the increasing frequency of its publication in literary journals that traditionally have not responded favorably to minority writers. Examples of these journals are: *Antaeus, North American Review, Poetry, Quarry West, The Spoon River Quarterly, Prairie Voices, The Denver Review, American Literary Review, The Iowa Review, Zyzzyva,* and *The Ohio Review. The American Book Review* recently devoted part of its January-February 1990 issue to Chicano and Chicana writing.

   More than forty Chicano writers have won prestigious National Endowment for the Arts Writing Fellowships. Ana Castillo and Genaro González are 1990 recipients. Rudolfo Anaya, Jimmy Santiago Baca, and others have served as judges and readers for this competition. Alberto Ríos, a University of Arizona Creative Writing Program alumnus, received a coveted Guggenheim Fellowship in 1990, and Aristeo Brito was awarded the Western States Literary Award for his novel, *The Devil in Texas*. These are some tangible signs that contemporary Chicano literature, like African-American literature before it, has finally been accepted into the canon of American letters.

   The most dramatic manifestation of Chicano literature's health and vigor is, for me, the overwhelmingly enthusiastic response to the call for manuscripts for this anthology and the subsequent necessity for future volumes. Thanks in large measure to the dedication of several members of the anthology's editorial board—I particularly would like to recognize Francisco Alarcón, Gloria Anzaldúa, Sandra Cisneros, and Gary Soto for their tireless efforts—we received in a six-month period more than 250 submissions from poets, novelists, dramatists, essayists, and short story writers. While often it was difficult to write rejection letters and choose between several excellent selections, it has been most heartening to know that there are hundreds of Chicano authors or would-be authors busily creating literature all over the United States. Submissions were received from Massachusetts, New York City, Washington, D.C., Minneapolis, and Kansas City as well as from Texas, New Mexico, Arizona, Colorado, and California.

   A word about language. While the great majority of the writers whose works appear in these pages have chosen English as their preferred language of creative expression, a few are more comfortable writing in Spanish, and yet others experiment with a fascinating alternation between the two languages. In some instances where works appear bilingually, the writers have provided their own translations. In a few cases, parts of narratives and poems were not translated; we chose to respect the writers' preference that the Spanish stand alone. We were not always guided by consistency but by the desire to let the anthology reflect the linguistic complexity and variety of contemporary Chicano literature.

The selections offered in *New Chicano Writing* demonstrate in fact that Americans of Mexican descent have an ever-growing awareness of themselves as a community and of their complicated but rightful place in American culture. The political *grito* of former years has articulated itself into the many literary forms and voices herein. This volume also raises issues inherent in a society dominated for too long by one culture, and balances them with both tradition and aesthetic sophistication. One of the most surprising and enlightening facets of new Chicano writing is the quality and volume of work by Chicanas. The boundaries of literature are indeed being tested by these works, which challenge preconceptions, draw on tradition, invent new forms and languages, question borders between race, class, and gender, and redefine what is canonical and what is marginal. The book's epigraph from Pat Mora's poem "The Young Sor Juana" speaks to this idea of artistic exploration and identification.

I am proud to be a part of this very exciting and personally gratifying project because it reaffirms once again my faith, ignited almost twenty-five years ago, that Chicano literature would become a major cultural phenomenon in American letters. It is a chorus of voices that is becoming louder and more finely tuned in its collective affirmation that Americans of Mexican descent are on the cutting edge of artistic expression in this country.

ALICIA GASPAR DE ALBA

Juana Inés

*Bless me, Padre, for I have sinned; my last confession was on
All Soul's Day. Forgive me for not going to the confessional,
but I couldn't speak this sin out loud, Padre, and I may not,
may never, be able to speak it in writing. Punish me, Padre,
as you would punish the vilest sinner, but don't make me say
this to you. Pull out my tongue, Padre, poke out my eyes,
lock me up in a convent. Do what you will, just don't make
me speak. I beseech the most pure, the most benevolent, our
Lady of Guadalupe, to save me from this ugliness. Hide me
under your robe, dear Lady, crush me under your feet like a
serpent.*

"Open this door, Juana Inés, or I shall have one of the ma-
sons take it down," said la Marquesa from the other side of
the barricaded door. "What is the matter with you, girl? Do
you have the pox that you quarantine yourself in this way?"

But Juana Inés could not answer. She dropped the quill on
the parchment and felt the ugliness swell within her, spilling
out of her eyes like innocent tears.

"I understand that you must be afraid, Juana," called la
Marquesa. "But the Viceroy and the professors are waiting for
you in the hall. You don't want to shame the palace, do you?"

If only you knew about me, thought Juana Inés, about this
love, this sin I cannot confess. But la Marquesa was right.
If she refused to participate in the tournament, the palace
would be put to shame, and she could not let her ugliness
contaminate the Viceroy's plans.

"I have an outstanding idea, Señora," the Viceroy had announced to his wife one evening over churros and hot chocolate. "The palace is going to sponsor a tournament between our brilliant Juana Inés and the most erudite members of the university. I'll call together professors from every field—theology, music, poetry, philosophy, mathematics, even astronomy—and we'll challenge them to find a gap in Juana Inés's education."

"But I'm only eighteen, your grace," Juana Inés had tried to dissuade him, "and nothing but a lady-in-waiting. Surely I have not learned enough to participate in such a contest."

"Nonsense," the Viceroy had said. "If you can answer their questions the way you play chess, I am certain that you will astonish and outwit them all. Don't be modest, Juana Inés; I can't abide modesty in an intellect like yours."

Again, la Marquesa ordered her page to pound on Juana Inés's door.

"Yes, my lady," Juana Inés answered la Marquesa's entreaties at last, "I am on my way."

"Thank God you have recovered your senses, girl. Do hurry. The professors are already finished with their dinner. I'm afraid you won't have time to eat, Juana."

"I'm not hungry, my lady," called Juana Inés, holding the confession she had just written over the flame of a candle. She opened her wardrobe and gazed at her fine gowns, all gifts from la Marquesa, but she could not wear anything that would stimulate the ugliness and distract her. In this contest, the only thing that mattered was her memory; her body and face were inconsequential, and so she would wear the plainest gown, the black one with the white lace collar and the ivory buttons.

In the mirror, her eyes looked as though she had rubbed them with prickly pears, and her skin was the color of maguey pulp. She poured water into the basin and wet her hair. She would braid it simply, with a black ribbon and would wear no jewelry, not even the cameo that her mother had sent her when she came to live at the palace, and certainly not the earrings or the necklace that la Marquesa had given her for her seventeenth birthday. She pushed the heavy bureau away from the door, expecting la Marquesa's page to be waiting for her, but the gallery was empty except for slave girls draping cloths over the bird cages.

Inhaling and exhaling slowly to loosen the muscles in her throat, Juana Inés walked to the great hall where the contest was to be held, thinking not of the questions that would be put to her—deep in her mind, she knew that the Viceroy's faith in her intellect was not unfounded—but of the first time she had performed in the great hall, the first time she had laid eyes on Leonor Carreto, Marquesa de Mancera.

"The Viceroy has summoned Juana Inés to the palace!" her uncle nearly shouted. "Listen to this, María: 'Esteemed don Juan de Mata: the Vicereine, la Marquesa de Mancera, requests the honor of making your niece's acquaintance. The court is anxious to meet the girl scholar who is stirring the talk of Mexico City.'"

"Oh my God," said her aunt María.

It was true that Juana Inés had been studying ever since she was three, that she had taught herself Latin grammar, geometry, and astronomy, that she had studied Greek philosophy and Roman law, but she did not consider herself a scholar, much less a prodigy as some chose to call her to the utter horror of her guardians who daily expected the Inquisition to accuse them of harboring a heretic in their midst. But the gossip flowed from the servants, and the city buzzed with the novelty of a girl who could read the constellations as easily as music.

"It's unnatural for a girl to know as much as you do, Juana Inés," her aunt had often admonished her. "You should learn how to embroider, how to crochet, like your cousins; those are safe things for girls to know."

Juana Inés did not argue with the Matas, but she knew that her wits would not be threaded through the eye of a needle. Her mind was the very pattern that the needle and thread tried to follow, the very fabric without which the pattern would be useless.

On the day of the Viceroy's summons, her aunt altered one of her own silk dresses for Juana Inés, and packed a trunk with Juana Inés's things just in case the Viceroy intended to offer her a position at the palace. The following morning, her uncle escorted Juana Inés to the court in his finest carriage. Juana Inés was sixteen. She had survived the ridicule and torment of the Matas for eight years. The idea of living at court, even if just to scrub the floors of the palace, was like a miracle to her. Surely there would be a library of exceptional quality at the court. Surely the Viceroy would not fear the Inquisition.

In the great hall, with the sunlight arching across the marble walls, Juana Inés glued her gaze to the Vicereine's eyes and pleaded silently to be taken in, to be saved from the ignorance of the Matas. The Viceroy twirled the ends of his thin mustache, his eyebrows raised as he studied Juana Inés's face.

"You say she taught herself Latin?" the Viceroy asked her uncle.

"And many other subjects as well, your Excellency. Juanita is a most studious girl. She impresses all of our friends with her conversation. Of course, we don't really understand why . . . "

"Does she play any musical instruments?" the Viceroy interrupted.

"Oh, she's quite a musician, your Excellency. She's an expert on the mandolin *and* the vihuela. She doesn't know much about sewing . . . "

Juana Inés's fingers had turned to wood. She knew what was coming next.

"We must have a demonstration," the Viceroy said, and snapped his fingers to the page standing at his side.

"Bring a mandolin from the music room," the Viceroy ordered. "Quickly."

The page bowed and scurried from the hall. Her uncle continued to extol her virtues as a musician but Juana Inés hardly heard him in her anxiety. She was trying to determine what would be the most appropriate thing to play. The piece had to be both modest and original, but it needed to live up to her uncle's praises, and so had to be . . . what was the best way to describe it? . . . haunting. She had to play the most haunting, most delicate piece she had ever written.

The Vicereine smiled at Juana Inés, leisurely fanning herself with a Chinese dragon.

"What will you play for us, Doña Ramírez de Asbaje?" the Viceroy asked Juana Inés.

"I would like to play one of my own compositions, if your majesties have no objection." The meekness in her voice surprised Juana Inés.

"No objections at all, my dear," the Vicereine spoke at last. "Does your composition have a name?"

The page scurried back into the hall.

"Hand it to the young lady," the Viceroy instructed the page. Juana Inés took the mandolin and fit the mahogany-and-spruce-striped belly of the instrument to her body, unable to resist caressing the sleek rose face. Inhaling the scent of the virgin wood, she tuned the strings, aware of the significance of this performance, aware of the Vicereine's eyes, of the jeweled buckles on the Viceroy's shoes, of her uncle's nervous breathing.

"Juanita, the Marquesa asked you the name of this composition?" her uncle said.

Juana Inés raised her head and looked at the Vicereine. "I call it 'The Cell,' my lady. That's the name of the room where I was born in my grandfather's hacienda."

"How very bizarre," said the Vicereine.

Juana Inés filled the sacks of her lungs with air. With her left hand she clasped the neck of the mandolin. With her right she removed the plectrum from between the strings and started to play. She had written the piece in the dark morning of her fifteenth birthday, upon awakening from a dream: Her grandfather stood on a riverbank in a circle of light, leaning against a bishop's crook. To reach him, Juana Inés had to float across the river on her back, arms over her head, but when she reached the light, it was a woman—not her mother or either of her sisters—a strange woman waiting on the riverbank, holding a black shawl. "Where's my abuelo?" Juana Inés asked. The woman said, "Don't be afraid. You're safe now."

When she awakened from the dream, she could hear this music in her head. The notes carried the delicacy of baptism and the mystery of death, and so she had called it 'The Cell.' Her mother had given birth to her in that room, and eight years later her grandfather had died there.

Juana Inés plucked the last few notes, then set the instrument down on her lap and kept her eyes on the Vice-reine's face.

"Excelentísimo," said the Viceroy, tapping the fingers of one hand into the palm of the other. Beside him, the Vice-reine stared at Juana Inés in a way that she could not decipher, a way that made her heart beat with a question that she had no words for.

"We have heard that you are quite a conversationalist," the Viceroy was saying to her, "that you can talk about any subject put to you. Is that true?"

Juana Inés said to the Viceroy: "I doubt I know as much as you, your Excellency; I am a girl, after all, and have not had the benefit of a formal education. I have read quite a few books, I guess. I have a good memory."

"If this girl had her choice between eating and reading, she would be a skeleton by now," said her uncle. "Why, she even renounced cheese . . . "

"She will not have to make that choice here," the Viceroy replied, smiling at Juana Inés under the tails of his mustache. "Would you like to stay at the palace, Juana Inés, and be a lady-in-waiting to la Marquesa?"

"Sir, I would be a slave to la Marquesa," Juana Inés answered, the relief in her voice thick as powder.

"Well, Señora Marquesa," the Viceroy turned to his wife. "Do you have an opinion to offer?"

"I believe you have made a wise decision, Husband," said the Vicereine, closing her fan and tilting her head to one side as if to study Juana Inés from a different angle. "I am sure Juana Inés will be quite an inspiration to me."

Juana Inés looked down and tried to keep her chin from shaking, but she could not control the tears of gratitude that streaked her face and slipped through the strings of the mandolin.

"And *I* believe the girl is baptizing the mandolin," said the Viceroy, chuckling. Juana Inés jumped up and tried to dry the instrument with her silk sleeve.

"Never mind," the Viceroy told her. "It's yours, to continue enchanting la Marquesa."

The chamberlain and his assistant were serving cups of hot chocolate to the professors and the guests seated in the great hall. The noblest hidalgos and their families had been invited to witness the contest, and among them sat Padre Antonio, the court's father confessor and spiritual adviser, the kind of priest who, it was rumored, knelt to the whip as passionately as to the cross and stained the walls of his quarters with his own blood. Juana Inés felt exposed. Surely the ugliness in her soul would be apparent to Padre Antonio. For an instant, she felt her memory and everything she had learned and stored inside it evaporate in the heat of her fear.

"There you are, Juana Inés!" said the Viceroy, getting to his feet as she entered the hall. "Gentlemen, it is my supreme pleasure to introduce you to the court's protégée, the Vicereine's friend and companion, Doña Juana Inés Ramírez de Asbaje."

Juana Inés stood beside the bench that had been placed in front of the audience and curtsied. "Forgive me for keeping you waiting; I have not been well," she said, her voice trembling.

"Should we postpone the tournament, Juana?" asked the Viceroy.

"I would not want the professors to think that I am surrendering without a struggle," she answered, sitting down. "I am quite ready to begin, thank you, Sir."

"Very well," said the Viceroy, turning to face the audience. "Esteemed ladies, noble gentlemen, as you know, we are here to test our protégée's education, which, as you also know, she has gained without the aid or direction of teachers. We shall see if our dignified professors can find a gap in Juana Inés's education, or, indeed, if Juana Inés will find a gap in theirs."

One of the professors in the audience guffawed into the velvet puff of his sleeve.

"Señor López," said the Viceroy. "Since you are in such a sanguine humor today, I will give *you* the honor of asking the first question."

Juana Inés avoided the green light of the Vicereine's eyes but looked straight into Padre Antonio's line of vision to ascertain whether or not he knew about her secret. The priest nodded at her paternally, and Juana Inés felt her fear dissolve and her memory stir back to life. She knew that the paleness of her face and her red-rimmed eyes and her quivering voice betrayed her, made her seem the vapid, frightened girl whom the professors had come to patronize or to embarrass. But she was determined to win this contest; if she could only keep her logic intact and not feel like a monkey performing in the Plaza Mayor, her victory was certain.

"Doña Ramírez," the professor named López commenced, "I would be most honored to hear from your learned lips the five conditions of the solitary bird, according to San Juan de la Cruz."

Juana Inés closed her eyes and concentrated on the image of her diary, saw her hand copying out the very text that professor López was now asking her to repeat.

"He must fly to the highest peak; he must not be afraid of solitude; he must sing to the sky; his color must not be definitive; his song must be very soft. And I will add, Sir, though

you didn't ask me to expound upon this symbol, that San
Juan de la Cruz was talking about the human soul. I recorded
the passage in my diary because it was the first time I had
ever come across an idea that made me weep, and weeping,
Sir, is not my nature."

"What do you say, Señor López?" asked the Viceroy. "Has
she satisfied your curiosity?"

The professor pressed his lips together and nodded reluctantly. "I acknowledge your astute assessment of the girl's
memory, Excellency," he murmured.

"Next!" called the Viceroy.

An older professor with a long wig stood up.

"Ah, Don Jorge," said the Viceroy. "I trust your question
will prove somewhat more of a challenge to our protégée than
the last one."

"Once upon a time," the old man spoke, his voice like a
bullfrog's croak, "the art of poetry along with all the other
arts were considered nothing more than imitation, artifices
that imitated the one true art. What can you tell us about
that, young lady?"

The contest allowed Juana Inés to confirm what she had always suspected of her mind: it was divided into two diametri-
cally opposite halves. While she exercised the side that contained the knowledge she had gleaned from her studies to
answer the professors' questions, in the other half of her
mind, she was imagining the confession that she would never
be able to make to Padre Antonio.

Bless me, Father, for I have sinned a deep and horrible sin, the
blackest sin.

"If you would be so kind, Doña Ramírez, as to construct a
syllogism for us, please."

There is love in my heart, Father, but it is a vile love, an unnatural, unnameable love, and yet, so deep, so pure.

"Have you any scholastic, or even scientific, evidence, Doña Ramírez, for this quaint conjecture of yours that women can aspire to the same mental and spiritual dimensions as men?"

I have violated the Vicereine's kindness, Father. I have sullied her with my ugliness.

"Perhaps our illustrious audience would enjoy listening to you recite a passage from *Don Quixote*, Doña Ramírez? I had in mind the old knight's monologue upon his strange enchantment."

I help her bathe. I braid her hair. I pour her chocolate. I wait on her, as I am supposed to do, Father, as her other ladies do. But none of them, I know, are tainted as I am. They grumble among themselves about how willful she is, how bad-tempered she is, how she treats them no better than slaves.

"Doña Ramírez, would you define mathematics for us, please, and explain Euclid's contribution to the field as well as the Archimedean principle?"

I know they're right, Father, but I don't blame her. She's an artist trapped in a woman's body; I understand her. I love her.

"You were speaking earlier of the nature of light and spiritual illumination, Doña Ramírez. Let us now examine the subject of light in a less esoteric, more mundane manner. I am alluding, of course, to the sun and will ask you, specifically, albeit circumlocutiously, about Copernicus. What theory did Copernicus propose that caused such an uproar in the Holy Office?"

I was not always aware of how I felt, Father. It came upon me last week, while we were . . . while I was . . . we were in the garden. La Marquesa was doing a sketch she wanted to call "Athena among Calla Lilies," and she had me posing for her in a yellow sheet fashioned to resemble a Greek tunic. She had snapped a calla off its stem and tucked it behind my ear, and I suggested to her that, as the patroness of war, Athena would probably not wear flowers in her hair. I tried to convince her to change the title of the sketch to "Aphrodite Among Calla Lilies," but she laughed at my suggestion. That would lack originality, Juana Inés, she said. Everyone expects the goddess of love to be surrounded by flowers, not the goddess of wisdom and patroness of war. I want to depict Athena as she might have been without the armor, a lithe, carefree, voluptuous Athena, unburdened by thoughts of war, innocent yet succulent, like the callas.

"Doña Ramírez, how would you explain the influence of the zodiac on a person's character and destiny?"

And then her Excellency made a comment about the color yellow, about how it set off the hazel flecks in my eyes and removed the melancholic pallor of my skin. I never noticed what an expressive mouth you have, Juana Inés, la Marquesa said, and my knees buckled, Father. I don't know, it may have been la Marquesa's unusual description of the lilies that disarmed me, that made me so susceptible to the sound of her voice, or perhaps the sun had been beating on my head too long (we *had* been out there all morning), but I started to feel very confused. I felt an attack of vertigo coming on, and my whole body itched as though I had just been attacked by a swarm of bees. I had to sit down. Her Excellency was most alarmed; she blamed herself for causing me what she interpreted as sunstroke, and immediately called one of the maids to bring a fan and a pitcher of water. She had me move to the grape arbor where it was cool and shady, and she actually fanned me, herself, crooning to me as though I were her own daughter. But it was not a daughterly feeling that I was feeling, Father. And it was not a daughterly instinct that made me lay my head on her breast and intoxicate myself with her closeness. Father, I'm so ashamed. So frightened. I love her so much.

"I didn't quite hear that, Doña Ramírez?"

"Forgive me, Sir," said Juana Inés, realizing that she had wandered too far into that dangerous hemisphere of her mind where logic had no roots. "Would you repeat the question, please? I suppose I'm getting rather tired."

"Of course you are, my dear," said the Vicereine. Turning to the Viceroy, she added, "Perhaps, Husband, we have seen enough. I, myself, am convinced that what I have witnessed here today is the equivalent of a royal galleon fending off the bothersome arrows of a few canoes."

"Yes, Madam, an exquisite analogy," said the Viceroy, "but I should like to hear our galleon's response to that last question. Do proceed, Professor de la Cadena."

"I was asking our girl scholar if she had any idea what the letter O symbolized to that very advanced, though admittedly pagan, culture of the Mayan people?" said the professor, who had gotten to his feet and stood with his fists at his waist, staring at Juana Inés with a palpable disdain.

"As you know, Sir, there is not much written about the history and philosophy of ancient México," said Juana Inés, "but in my grandfather's hacienda where I grew up, there was an old Mayan gardener who told me a story about three sacred letters; I believe they were the T, the G, and the O. She was a very old woman and I a very young girl, starving for stories. Unfortunately, all I remember of that story is this: once upon a time, there was a great and blessed tree known as the Tree of Life that grew as high as the Milky Way, the spiral path through which the gods traveled, through which existence unfolded, and the fruit of this tree was the human mind, ripe and round as a pomegranate, its seeds filled with what she called The Nothing and The Everything."

"Enough of this pagan chattering!" a voice called out. It

was Padre Antonio, who was now also on his feet behind the Viceroy and la Marquesa, his face white as bone. "The zodiac! The tree of life! The spiral path! I'm shocked, your Excellency, that you have permitted this girl to spice her studies with arcane reading!"

"Scandalous!" said Professor de la Cadena.

"A royal galleon, indeed!" the Viceroy said, applauding. The rest of the audience followed suit, but Juana Inés could sense that the air between their palms had become as taut as her own vocal chords.

"We have a guitar trio waiting in the patio, everybody," announced the Vicereine.

Pretending to ignore their shifty glances and shaking heads, Juana Inés watched them—the murmuring señoras, the indignant caballeros—follow la Marquesa through the glass doors of the salon. She had expected la Marquesa to felicitate her in some way: a kiss, an embrace, even a smile. But she had not so much as looked at Juana Inés, and Juana Inés felt paralyzed on her bench, abandoned. Two meters away the Viceroy and Padre Antonio were arguing about her education.

"How can she know if something is forbidden when she has no teachers?" the Viceroy asked.

"As censor for the Holy Office, your Excellency, I must report the girl. Her soul is in danger of excommunication if she continues with these heretical studies."

"Let us be reasonable, Padre Antonio. You have known for as long as the girl has lived at the palace that she is an omnivore of books and that she has mnemonic capacities of magnanimous proportions. Is it her fault that she remembers things she shouldn't? Will the Holy See excommunicate a young girl for having a good memory?"

"Joan of Arc was roasted at the stake for listening to angels," said Padre Antonio, "and she was the same age as Juana Inés."

The black magnet of Padre Antonio's eyes pulled Juana Inés's gaze away from the lace collar of her dress.

"Look at her, your Excellency," said the priest. "She knows

she has wronged God and our Mother Church, do you not, Juana Inés? Come here, Child. We must speak of the future of your soul."

Juana Inés walked like a somnambulist toward Padre Antonio, her victory over the professors dragging behind her, heavy as a cross.

"Please forgive me, my dear," the Viceroy said. "I had no idea the tournament would result in this. I trust that Padre Antonio," and at this the Viceroy cast a sidelong sneer at the priest, "will not condemn my soul if I congratulate you for a performance that not only exceeded my wildest expectations but also increased my admiration for your talents, and, I'm sure, won you the respect of your colleagues; for, despite your sex and your age, you are, indeed, their colleague, my dear."

From the courtyard came the keening of the guitars. The Viceroy lifted her hand to his lips and brushed his mustache over her fingers. When he had gone, Padre Antonio raised his right hand over Juana Inés' face. She flinched, expecting the priest to strike her, but he only drew a cross in midair, her doom or her salvation.

"I know you are no heretic, Child. And I understand the Viceroy's point about your memory and your voracious appetite for books. I have, therefore, a proposition to make, a way of directing your mind toward higher learning while saving your soul at the same time. How would you like to be a bride?"

"Marriage?" screeched Juana Inés.

"The ultimate marriage," said the priest, his eyes glittering like flints of obsidian.

She closed her eyes and imagined a man's hands on her body. A man's lips and beard on her face. Her belly swelling with children. Her mind shriveling like a prune. "Oh, no, Father!" she cried, clutching at his wide sleeves, "please, don't make me get married. I'd rather burn at the stake like Joan of Arc. Please, Father."

"An earthly marriage is not what I mean. In that black dress, I see a humble and obedient bride of Christ, of the Carmelite order, perhaps. *Yes*, the Carmelites will cleanse that vanity of yours that has led you into dangerous waters."

"Carmelites, Father?" Juana Inés felt her lungs contract in her rib cage.

Padre Antonio looked up at the candles in the chandelier and made the triple sign of the cross. "I see, now, the infinite wisdom of your plan, oh Lord," Padre Antonio seemed to chant.

"But I'm registered as a daughter of the church, Padre," said Juana Inés. "I have no father, no dowry; I could never be a nun. I'm . . . " what was she? . . . What else could she be? . . . "I'm a sinner, Padre."

"Of course you are, my daughter," said Padre Antonio, "of course you are."

JOEL HUERTA

LARGESSE

In the countryside sky
a smoke rises in the distance
like a truth, like a streak of gray
spilling from the mouth in the beard of a swami.

In the Bible belt the sun is a buckle,
a swami is a kook.

Yet this time the countryside and its pillar of smoke
placates us and the blue space around it,
overreaches into our own hunger,
our own black grass pitching about.

We've stopped to eat vacation sandwiches,
we eat up the experience and all,
because more is needed just now
to convince that living is more than punishment.

Because we're not from here,
because we've parked our Chevette,
fixed sandwiches on the hood.
Because we gawk and chew in love with ourselves
—*you have never looked this good, brother*—
we eat.

Because where one is not from is
where larger knowledge plants her foot,
one drives there, we've stopped here
in this large country

and find we reacquaint ourselves
with ourselves . . . *hello.*
We cannot help it.

And I'm not unlike you,
I take souvenirs when I travel:
the low huisache tree,
the white-wing egg coddled and
returned to the crotch of a tree,
the prickly pear's pear dyeing your chin scarlet
is a love story our mother tells
of being poor and using berries as lipstick,
then a kiss.

I take the grass, I take the dog barking,
the snowbirds in RVs going south like aged elephants.
I take you.
I take the roadside cross's magenta elegy,
I take the grass immediately around it,
the carcrash dead of all the highways,
the windshield quartz of wrecks—they go with me.

I am glad
we've stopped here, brother,
and not at Dairy Queen.
I will tell you this later
after that phrase of smoke, this sandwich,
this bliss.

SPLENDID DUTY

FOUR ADOLESCENTS LAUGHING
on the walkway
hurry toward a paradise,

though they themselves
—roughhousing—constitute
paradise, and—not knowing—ignore it,
sing along.

> IT KNOCKS YOU ON YOUR ASS
> this heretofore quietest
> of afternoons, when you realize
> the young ones don't want to be you.

IT KNOCKS YOU ON YOUR ASS
why that peach fuzz dagger
on the kid's upper lip
is there to lance
hearts like your own, like mine.

> THOSE TOMATOES THEY SQUASHED
> on the sidewalk trail, of course, like blood
> to yonder garden;
> the horse of afternoon has run,
> and school's-out-for-summer papers
> tumble but catch on fences.

SOUTH TEXAS MINIMAL

In the photograph I was unable to get
this summer, the horizon would stretch cleanly
across the frame—a razor cut
opening-out to somewhere else.
Last summer, I was in love
with a woman, and then in July
I loved the secret movement of the stingray.

That summer Horizon was an afterthought:
a skillet which cooked sunset,
or "the place to sail to . . . ."

This summer I make my home here
and so this Laguna Madre horizon is suddenly
significant—being the shelf
in the roof of South Texas, which holds.

In this photograph I was unable to get,
the portrait of my landscape
is just fine: clean lines, water smooth
(the lovely curved ass of the world).

Like my mother knows about foaling colts,
like brother believes in dolphins,
I suppose that's the way
I want to know my landscape.
Last summer, I caught fourteen stingrays,
and this summer yields not one empty photograph.
In one frame a black skimmer splits
light on the water veil.
Another shot shows a fine horizon,
but in the foreground where I hope for nothing
there's a mullet,
in the next, there's the splash;
and this photo says *mullet*, not *horizon*.

LOWRIDER CAR

Shipwrecked on our weekends and ourselves,
we bolt the chrome angel to the nose
of our Ford Brougham, and with that angel,
I think, contract *Beauty* to remain

beyond our payday and what has always been recorded
in the Book of Knowledge as the simpleton's
numb transport through twilight toward darkness.

As we pass by you, our heads trailing in the blue
of ornamental wings (as in night
postcards of vehicles enstreamed, head and taillights standing
for the individual, awhir in the circuitry of the uncloaked
city) I hear your voice.

I hear it on the white quietly symbolic journeys
of tufty milkweed pods in the current
American method of using lesser-known weeds
in place of fated, undistillable rose,

I hear you say you hear
our car iron forward in the left-turn lane
with ourselves, hear you ask what spirit,
blinking its plastic wing, is so maddened
(red robed through The Milky Way),
and what stubborn course to *Beauty* she sponsors.

WALMART AMERICA QUARTET

We did not, in fact, come to the United States.
The United States came to us.   Luis Valdés

Humdrum Pageants

On the way there the cat, The Indio,
stepped in Jackie's mouth,
and she cried like in that moment
in the Japanese film
where the geisha smiles,
but reveals a mouth bleeding,

so the helicopter-mounted camera
abandons her in the landscape,
and the credits roll up,
and you see her real name.

Having lost his footing,
and so banished
to the cargo hold of our little ship,
The Indio clawed at the windows of our wagon,
and you standing by the highway
hitchhiking for a life,
see The Indio and are reminded
how we all suffer
—how apparent that given becomes
—recall the geisha
the plenty of times
where we felt it could have been us,
translated there to those other
even more humdrum pageants
—recall
the hapless tolling of porch lights in towns
—the hapless tolling of lights
one threads as precious beads,
It could have been us.

Ozzy

I said, "There's the Alamo, and there's the plinth
with our heroes which died to free us from the Mexicans,
and there's where Ozzy Osborne bit the head off a dove,
and that's where he pissed." Remember the Alamo.

Honda Automotive, a Dream

It went like that till early morning
when pink homey curtains

blew out a double-wide trailer window
in WIDE LOAD tow.

The housing unit was transferred in halves,
and being so much like a cracked egg,
it got us dreaming again.
Like a hooker's frenetic tongue
to the eye on the fraternity boy,
whose chemistry has marched him to her,
the passing curtains set ablaze
our desire to be local
—to where we are fixed on a yard
drinking blush wine,
our cheeks flushed from the more bountiful
wine of twilight,
through which our offspring
play tag on All-Terrain-Vehicles,
wherein I say:

> *Yep, that's the way Honda Automotive*
> *got started, Honey, three-wheelers,*
> *then econoboxes, now handsome*
> *cars, cars like our own Accord.*

WalMart Discount City

When we awoke,
the exclamation points of rain
were in the distance—a party
of fishing lines hoisting-up Discount City.

Hondas and Suburbans emerged,
washed & waxed from the mirage,
heading to where
The Indio lay buried
by the fruit tree

of trailer house pleasure,
trailer court doom.

The Texas Department of Public Safety wildflowers
monogrammed the wool of summer, yes,
appeased the future,
sustained the very highway.

GULF OF MEXICO, FIREWORKS

Clouds stuck
on the scene like cataracts,

last night
and I remembered . . .

other clouds had dawdled by
the night before

which could have been July 4th,
the way people were out,

and white-tailed deer (clouds) grazed
in the blue brush of sky

and you could say
the bottlerockets and each trail of sparks

were an arrow whose directrix
couldn't reach
or wound our deer.

I wish you could have seen it.

A couple walked along the water.
His trousers were rolled to the calf
like in a planned image she tugged.

And even though glass is not allowed on the beach,
he popped a champagne bottle,
the diver arced, I didn't see it.
their plastic glasses met,

I couldn't hear it,
but there were toasts proposed

to love and to dollars,
to the rainy deer in the sky,

leaning toward Texas,
their tongues to the saltlick (our roused heads)
—their antlers blue with lightning.

—after Johnny Cash

SOME ANGEL, OR WINGED STAR

When I held you tight,
performing the Heimlich,
and picked you up,

I promised you,
I would never let you die,

and I'm sorry
as I see white doves
at your funeral

coocooing as they're shaken
from a coop,
when the eulogy is done

and the thrown roses,
cross-hatched, stacked,

like an unwinnable game of pick-up sticks
on the casket

and one bird
not wanting to fly the coop,
stays.

THE BEAUTY NOOK HAIR SALON, 1965

And it matters,
that the smile
        the beautician gives the boy's mother is real,
sincere,
that the boy is satisfied
        with his trimmed, combed hair,

that in the daylight, outside,
        a tomcat hypnotizes a cardinal
on a work truck antenna,

that Cosmonaut Leonov walks the snowy hood
        of a shifty, aquamarine earth,

that the beautician's German shears
        orbit the boy's mother's ratted 'do,

chord, like the hummingbird's zip
        above thorny bougainvillaea.

It matters that the boy's parents build
        a paper house
with the paychecks they've installed
in the savings and loan's dark Saturday vault.

And it matters that the beautician
is white,

her client is brown,
and that that doesn't matter.

Inside The Beauty Nook the sole client
        dissolves a root beer candy in her mouth.

At the window
        AIRCONDITIONING advertised
—little snows
        heaped atop letters.

Outside in the fickle nation,
        the white-haired farmers initiate a migration,
goodbye, Midwestern snow and elms.

The South Texan fidgety sky,
        the frazzled edge of the sunbelt,
the singular lives diffracting

—Chicanos and whites,
        tails between their legs,
stepping towards the other.

The heat and the wind and the jumbo drops of rain.

ODILIA GALVÁN RODRÍGUEZ

MUD BOY

I

when I see you
I double take.
you miniature man.
resembling the only one I ever loved
grand canyons deep.

in my soft red earth,
chamisa and cactus
spotted desert depths,
in eight short months
you formed,
little mud boy.

the greatest diviner tapped
early into your source.
you sprang to my surface
slowly at first. then a geyser
gushing and gliding
new life of immense force.

with ease you gurgled stories
about the depths from where you'd come.
with your chubby tree limbs you learned
to crawl. then after many spills and falls
balancing on shaky new legs you got up
and walked. soon bird coos became words.

in the black whirlpools of your little eyes
I remembered how to love myself again.

    II
we read books like other
kids eat candy. you know
Puff the Magic Dragon
as though he lived next door.
The Wild Things are always
roaming the weed-trees in our
backyard turned forest.

we are Indians
brave and proud.
thankful to cowboys
for only one thing,
they brought back
the mighty horses
we ride
at fire engine speed.

while the man-made storms
of the last two years
circled my world
joining hands   singing
you and I played
ring around the rosy
turning and skipping clockwise.

laughing at la Pelona
I refused to fall down.

MURALIST

to Jane

sandia red
elote yellow
lupine purple
cobalt blue
colors
paint you
life in love
and struggle

before spring greens
there was a time
when even mauve orange
and green golden
Santa Cruz sunsets
couldn't make you smile

but now
amongst pavement blacks
gray-blue and steel
your power and strength
radiates clear
a prism

neon magenta
fuchsia, sky blue,
desert ochre,
cloud white, and the rest
shoot from your fingertips
transmuting blank-faced walls
    into sirens for peace

SEQUOIA SEMPERVIRENS

you talked to me
in a walking dream
in the Sinkyone wilderness
I know many of you were
massacred with the buffalo
with the People

you showed me the stumps
loggers left
relatives standing
like grave stones
amputees
then the circles
of trees
which grew from
sprouts
around them

you told me that
you're still
very young
don't become
grown up
until you're four
or five hundred
years old
it was the ancients
they cut down

you said
when the grasses
come back
and the roads are

put to bed
so will the owl
the chipmunk
the mink
big cats
condors and bear

when the prairie and
trees come back
so will the buffalo
so will
we.

MIGRATORY BIRDS
to Antonia

you were born
to gypsies
though you didn't
want to be
every spring
when orange blossom's
perfume
filled the air
your world was packed
into a few bundles
then your
family was off
living in tents
trailers
dirt floor shacks

you were born
to nomads
though you didn't
want to be
longed to live
with the
settled and the straight
work in the
five-and-dime
go to school
play tennis
and every time
you found a friend
it was time to go
another town
another round
in a world
that made you
dizzy

you were born
to migrants
though you didn't
want to be
from Texas to Illinois
living a blur
out a car window
roads endless
as fields of crops
to be picked by the piece
never making enough
to eat
let alone for the trip back
home

pleading for the
traveling to stop
words in the wind
wooshing by ears
of the gypsy king

you were born
to wanderers
though you didn't
want to be
when you got
the chance
you planted
yourself
deep
in concrete
and steel
to make sure
you or your
offspring
wouldn't
branch out
too far
from home
you were
settled
for
ever

I was born
to a life of never change
though I didn't
want to be
same familiar streets

same people
same stories
year after year
until one sweltering
Chicago summer night
the moon full
color of sun
reflecting off
fields of green
and the sweet scent
of lilacs from
our backyard
helped me sprout wings
so I could fly away.

LUIS OMAR SALINAS

BAREFOOT WITH A ROSE

I blame tequila
and a rose,
my shoeless romance
of the sky . . .
I blame the schizophrenic
whose chatter I couldn't
deal with.
I blame my comfortable
treatises on the existence
of love
I blame the voyeurs crouched
in the shade of cemeteries
and the highs and lows
of madness.
I blame the fact
that there's no one
there to forgive
my foolishness.

TO OUR AMIGOS

The potted plants
as if awaiting death,
the trailer parked,

and the night
dense, thick
with boredom.

A friend I haven't seen
for years visits.
I show him to the den
where I do my writing
and we drink Chenin Blanc
as if fate had
made a mistake
and we had become genteel.

I thank him for a poem
dedicated to me,
the one in which lilacs
are as immortal as clouds,
in which I stroll by a lake
in a white, three-piece
summer suit, sharing bites
of my sandwich with the swans
once I have become
recognized and am living
almost comfortably in Chicago.

We drink to the absent
and there is no despair,
no fear—there is finally
only the moonless night
beneath which we drink
to our amigos
and a forlorn Muse.

NIGHT WALTZ

The night begins
with its
blind tap dancers
in the fog, ghosts playing
cards in the moonlight.
This is the inner world
of a poet who
peers intently
through the haze.
All this could end
with a snap
of the fingers,
a kiss from
a luminous woman.

This is the madness
left over from evening,
come down from the moon—
bitten clouds and blue
tops of the elms
to haunt me.
This is the whirling
environment
of animals
in the half light.

With a little luck
the evening could
digress into
an interlude of violins,
into a sleeping woman
with a book of prayers
by her side.

Around all this,
the air whispers,
and children
circle
the mountain for home.

PIECES

The day goes by like a child
wandering through the woods
dropping his sandwich wrappers,
losing his way . . .
The spring air wraps itself
around two lovers in the meadow.
Rabbits and squirrels dash
to and fro
This is every excitement
of the day.
A mother waves goodbye
to her son
in a blossom of fingers,
and the sky
turns the color of dark
plums. The lovers part
brushing leaves and twigs
from their hair
as it starts to rain.
The child's mother
chews on death's ear.

The day collapses
on dark knees,

and a woman is heard
screaming in the distance—
this then must be
the beginning
of Purgatory?

GLORIA ANZALDÚA

Ghost Trap

A woman was building a ghost trap to catch the ghost of her
marido, who had recently died. She wanted to keep him from
coming into her house. At first she had been devastated by his
death. She had thrown herself into the grave on top of his cof-
fin wailing like *la llorona*, the ghost woman who wandered in
the dark. She would wake in the middle of the night in a sweat,
turn to him to share a dream or a fear and find an emptiness.
She would walk from room to room at night feeling like a
ghost. The loneliness turned into anger at his desertion.

One night the second week after his death she woke to find
him in bed with her, or rather his ghost. *"¡Viejo!"* she cried
out, smiling for the first time since his death. But suddenly
she frowned and felt fear squeeze her heart.

During the day he would follow her around the house and
to the backyard but he would never go beyond the front gate
when she left to run errands. She began to spend more time
away from the house. She realized that she missed her solitude. Instead of making her feel wanted and protected, as his
presence had before his death, his constant hovering now
stifled her.

"Viejo, why do you keep coming back every night? Did you
leave something unfinished? Is there some business you want
to complete? Tell me and I'll help you do it."

"Vieja, viejita linda, bring me clean clothes," he said to her
in a wisp of a whisper.

"Ba, estás muerto, ¿pa' qué necesitas ropa?" You're dead,
you have no need of clothes, she whispered back. His repeated
request, which seemed to get louder and louder, finally drove

her to the closet. Of course his clothes were missing; she'd given them away. Now she would have to go into the shop and buy men's things and face the look of censure in the shop-keeper's face at how fast she had replaced her husband with another man.

"Vieja, vieja, fix me some dinner," he said in a harsh mutter. She fixed him *carnitas*, his favorite dish, and set it on the table. But a ghost can't eat and the food sat on the table gathering flies. "Vieja, viejita linda, bring me a beer." Off she would go to the market to get the beer. *La gente* began to talk about how her grief had driven her to drink. She would pull the lid and place the can of beer on the table by "his" chair. "You know I only drink Dos Equis," he growled. The beer went flat. She was tempted to drink his beer to alleviate her increasing irritation.

Tending to his ghost seemed to take all her time. She began to resent all the washing and cooking and trimming of his hair and toenails when he was alive. Just when she thought herself free, the pisser was back and more trouble now that he was dead. Her only consolation was that she didn't have to wash his smelly socks and dirty underwear. But her two-week-old *vida* was no longer her own and she wanted it back. How could she stop her *marido muerto* from returning?

One day she got inspired. She made a little model of her house with Popsicle sticks and glue and placed it in a safe spot halfway between his grave in the nearby cemetery and her home. She had heard that ghosts don't have a sense of perspective. Rocking back and forth, her chair creaked on the porch as she waited for *el espanto* to enter the model house thinking it was the real one.

That night she did not awaken. In the morning when she woke, she turned toward the side where her husband had been sleeping the past thirty years. His ghost was not there, nor was he there the following night. She sat up waiting for him, worrying about what to do with the ghost house. Suppose someone found *la casita* and accidentally opened the door and let the ghost out. Conceivably some element of nature—a strong wind or a fire—could destroy the flimsy house and her dead husband could get out. The tiny house was too fragile to be buried—the earth would crush it and the ghost would escape. She had to put it somewhere safe and out of the reach of others. After several days of deliberation she carefully carried the ghost trap into her house and placed it under the bed where mischievous nieces and nephews could not find it. That night a voice woke her up. It called out, no longer whispering. *"Vieja, vieja quiero hacerte el amor."* She thought she felt his body stirring under the bedcovers. Half dreaming, half awake, she pushed him away, but he kept climbing on top of her. All night she refused to open her legs to him.

Next morning she woke with deep grooves down the corners of her mouth and bruises on her mouth, breasts, arms, and inner thighs. She peered under the bed and saw that the door of the *casita* was open. She walked from room to room looking for *el pinche desgraciado* and muttering to herself, How am I going to get rid of that fucker? She considered going to the local *curandera* and asking her to drive his soul into *el pozo*, better yet, to hell. Huh, or she could look through the yellow pages to find a ghostbuster. Ah, no, she'd do it herself—with words and curses.

She decided to be prepared should her words fail. That night she plugged in the vacuum cleaner and put it by her bed. She tugged on two of her sturdiest corsets, several pairs of pants and three shirts, turned off the lights, got into bed and waited. She jumped out of bed, fetched her heavy iron skillet and hid it under the bedcovers just in case he'd taken on more substance than the vacuum could handle. Come on *cabrón, vente chingón,* she said under her breath.

Puddles

For Rodrigo Reyes and Jaye Miller

The gay man always left a puddle on his chair, along with the tip on the table. It got so Prieta ceased being surprised. With one hand she'd wipe it up with a towel (the puddle wasn't very big) and with the other, pocket the quarter. The tip was always a quarter no matter whether it was coffee he'd ordered or a full meal. After half a dozen times of wanting to, Prieta finally dipped her finger in. The puddle, Prieta decided after sniffing it, was not piss. Nor was it water, though it looked clear. She put the wet finger in her mouth—it didn't taste like wine or coffee.

The next morning, as she washed her face she noticed that the tip of her tongue had turned green. She scrubbed it with her toothbrush. She rinsed it with mouthwash. No changes. She was running late for work. Never mind the green tongue. She planned to confront the man whose puddle had turned her tongue green. Was he carrying some weird disease? Come to think about it, he was a bit strange. Along with the pink triangle and earring in his left ear, he always wore an olive green parka that covered him to his knees. Though he never spoke to her, just pointed at the menu when he ordered, nodded or shook his head when she came around with the coffee carafe, a look of recognition would pass between them. Did he have a reason for always picking one of her tables instead of one of Amy's? Both were dykes, but Amy was the one who smiled and cracked jokes with the customers while Prieta complained about the twenty-five wars—imagine, twenty-five—being fought on the planet. Now that she thought about it, he always sat at the same table. *Jíjole, qué curioso.* How long had he been coming in? Two weeks?

"What's wrong with your finger?" asked her friend Amy when she got to *Les Amis.* "Why is it green?"

"My finger? ¡*Ayno!* she said looking at her finger and giving a small yipe.

"Would you believe I have a way with plants? *Tu sabes*, a green thumb?"

Amy looked at her funny. "You've never showed you've had a sense of humor—until now that is. Your face is all lighted up. You wearing some kind of fluorescent make-up? The color's all wrong, got sort of a greenish tinge. Oh, and your knees look sort of wrinkled," she said bending down to get a closer look. Prieta craned her head to look at her knees.

Though a voice called, "Oh, waitress," she snuck into the washroom and peered into the broken and dirty mirror over the sink. Yeah, her face looked different even though she couldn't pinpoint the changes. The green had begun to creep from her finger to the back of her hand.

All day as she bustled from table to counter to kitchen she kept an eye on the door. But the man who made puddles did not come in that day, nor the next. She noticed the customers kept eyeing her knees. *Su piel se convertía en cuerpo de lagarto.*

By the fourth day she *knew* what each customer was going to order before they opened their mouths. She also knew that the "green man" was never coming back—he didn't have to, he'd done his deed. On the fifth day she had to wear trousers, long-sleeved shirts that buttoned all the way to her neck and heavy beige make-up. But it was her gloved hands that cast suspicion on her, and at the end of the week, her boss told her he had to let her go because she was spooking the customers. By then she had only to cast her eyes over some man hunched over his lunch or dinner and she'd know if he was sticking it to his daughter. She would slap the check, along with a napkin, face down on the table. The bold green letters on the napkin would read, "I know what you are doing to your daughter. If you do it again your thing will turn green and fall off." By the end of the week she did not need this particular waitressing job. A few days later her green skin began to flake off. Underneath it she could see her original brown skin emerge. She began to get glimpses of other "afflicted" people—something in their eyes marked their difference.

She decided to drop by *Les Amis* to see if Amy was ready.

If she was, Prieta would leave her the gift and say good-bye. Prieta had found out what her real work was—to move from town to town, work in restaurants, keep her knees covered, and when no one was looking touch an exposed knee to a chair and let slide a puddle of tears.

ELBA SÁNCHEZ

LOS DESTERRADOS

larga es la espera
sin cobija
y el frío trasnochador
de tu tembloroso espíritu
ahora sombra adormecida
arriesga el calor de tu vida

oscuro es el portón
en que ahora te refugias
sin encontrar la puerta
la noche se abre en vuelo
y te sientes a punto de caer
en el precipicio

UPROOTED

Endless is the waiting
without cover
sleepless and cold
your trembling spirit
now dormant shadow
risking the heat of your life

dark is the gateway
in which you seek refuge
without finding a door

the night opens in flight
and you feel about to fall
into the abyss

PUEBLO PINTOR
a Isaías Mata y el pueblo salvadoreño

no borrarán la sangre
de los muros
de las calles
presente está allí
el lienzo vivo
de derramados rojos
púrpuras magentas

no callarán la voz
testigo cada vez
más fuerte
presente está allí
brocha en mano
creando imágenes
carnosidad de barro y verde

no disolverán el azúl
tu azúl favorito
fuerza vertida
de cielos
de valles
de miles de bocas
volcanes

LIVING CANVAS

for Isaías Mata and the Salvadoran People

they will not wipe away the blood
from the walls
the streets
it is there present
living canvas of spilled reds
purples magentas

they will not silence the voice
witness each time
ever louder
it is there present
brush in hand
creating images
proud flesh of clay and green

they will not dissolve the blue
your favorite blue
scattered force
of skies
valleys
of thousands
of mouths
volcanoes

ESPEJISMO: MUJER POESÍA

ésta no viene engalanada
vestida de encajes
ni tampoco viene
con pelos en la lengua
no

ésta no llega
adornada de florecitas
a rosa olorosa
no señor

ésta viene
vientre puño
piedra hueso
velo espuma
raíces tallos
manos brazos
espinas le curten
la lengua

a veces ofrece
hilos de miel
flor de naranjo
a veces
arroja veneno

ésta
ésta viene
a dar testimonio
a expresar su dolor
abriendo la puerta
a su realidad
gritando verdades
abrazando fuertemente
su pasión

MIRROR IMAGE: WOMANPOETRY

this one doesn't
stand before you
dressed in lace

nor does she come
mincing words
no
this one doesn't arrive
dressed in little flowers
smelling of a rose
no sir

this one comes before you
womb first
rock bone
veil foam
root offspring
arms hands
thorns pierce
her tongue

at times she offers honeyed threads
orange blossoms
at times
she flings poison

this one
this one comes
to give testimony
to express her pain
opening the door
to her reality
shouting truths
firmly embracing
her passion

BERNICE ZAMORA

Tere

O Tynnus,

By the grace of whoever administers grace, I breathe
the rhythm of dying scribes, those copiers of Bibles, century after century, that rhythmic consciousness that
aimed to avoid the rhythm of the vascular systems sensi-
tive to the forces of adrenalin and atomic waste. In other
words, this mind aimed to separate itself from this body's
world, the wordy world of Christmases, May Days, and
most of all the Grace Amazing Days of full-grown men
of bodies and bloods commingling. My rhythm is single-
celled pulsation with an occasional spasm to solitary
humming about the day at hand, each day presenting
$E = mc^2$ translations and occasional leaks in theories of
being. I served my need to serve a handsome Christ without understanding Old Testament Covenants, altared
symbols, or ancient religions of early, early Americans.
By instruction, I served those generations of teachers
who tested the truth of religious theories not at all,
teachers who, when inclined to generosity with Biblical
promptings of THE WORD, made it available jab by syl-
labic jab, whole constructs be damned, and by the grace
of the Christian God "be thankful the sun shines on you
at all, child," I recall a Bishop saying to us beggars of
confirmation. And so indeed, by the grace of administers
of grace, I breathe slowly and in time to a time unre-
corded, a time of creaturehood.

Thinking for myself is a new experience. I still don't
trust it. It may be I am thinking with an instrument

honed still to obey, a self-correcting instrument to be
called back after my probing mission is exhausted. Certainly, I am thinking in a language I did not create. In
my own language, thoughts, when I can identify them,
are fully three-dimensional colors, sometimes four-
dimensional colors of movements, movements of music
pitched to match the colors, colors to match the mood of
my thoughts, thoughts that are mine, territorially mine,
dimensionally mine, rhythmically my own feelings of
form and fission. These moments, these exquisite moments when I trust the foreign words, I can tell that I
have lived this life wrongly.

From what I can tell, this is the sixth day. The Gods
are not yet resting. We scribes are a reference to the form
of humanity. Each of us is called into the form in a special way, in a way of creativeness by telling one, then the
other, of the form in which we live; then we tell of the
Gods who are not yet resting. We become a chain of
happy dispatch this way, you see. I must presume happiness here because my silence in the chain of telling sheds
a different world from the others. I lived in the unseeing
world of B.C./A.D. limbo. All scripture was invisible to
me and the little physical baby body—the means by
which I was to tell my proclamation, was separated from
scripture at birth.

And I was separated from the others physically, bio-
logically, by sex. My silence predicated the separation.
My silence was perceived as rebellion against the Gods'
Mealy Mandate. To me silence seemed a safer companion
in the task of copying Bibles, and copying Bibles seemed
a better way to pass the telling than to get married.

I refused, you see.

Fortunately, Three Gods agreed to instruct me in the
joys of coupling and commitment so I would not crush
the stubborn creature. And they agreed to instruct in the
collective; that is, they agreed among themselves to in-

struct me three at a time, three gods at a time. None
willed to instruct me face on, one on one, not one. It's
the old language problem. Semantics. Love for Human-
kind vs. Love for Man vs. Female Survival. Well, you
know the old camps. And then there's passion. How does
passion comfort silent scribblers of the Bible? Alas, I am
the last female of the dying scribes, and I am to choose
whether to die without hope of scripture or I am to
marry with the happy reward of my own language for
the telling.

I distrust the bargain.

Yes, I have lived this life wrongly. And insanity did not
embrace me as it so kindly embraced the others. Rather,
a willfully, uplifting existence of inspiring goodness acti-
vated in this life more tortures than are contained in the
Catholic hell. I exaggerate the case the Gods tell me.
Hardly, I responded. Believe me, all the tragedies that fell
on me were entirely against my will. And having done
unto others as I would have them do unto me since early
childhood, I did myself embrace the doctrine of defeat.
"Nonsense," the Gods reverberated, "nothing can happen
against your will."

Perhaps. Still, the will to do good acts and to be a good
person gripped my heart with the stranglehold of the
ages. The desire itself predated the age of reason and
choice. Some newborn scribes, especially, are predisposed
to goodness. Choice and reason enter that child's trek
through tragedies much too late to connect the will to do
good with the will to tragedy. "I was indeed bound and
dragged to tragedy against my will!" I shouted to the
Gods. Small wonder they placed me among the tribe of
Aztlán.

It was hardly an arbitrary law that directed I should
be born into a community of cruel poverty and after the
splendor was plundered, too. The highest intelligence
created this situation and the Mandate I am to conclude
before my language is fully restored. The Gods them-

selves created and enlivened paralyzing days stretching
memory back twelve centuries, as the raven crowed. The
moment of birth stretched into one such day. I recall it as
stark whiteness, chill, and shock, as if the winter's snow
outdoors had been transported indoors. My arrival in
January was to a religious household, one of annoyance
and inconvenience. Every, literally every, remarkable in-
cident of my life proved to be equally and exceedingly
ill-timed.

I don't wish to be blasphemous, but the Holy Three,
the Adamant Holy Three, are flirting with the coward's
corn. Three at a time indeed. My, my. Why not assign
one God to me as has been done for the others? Discussion with one God is easier, and there's no mocking from
the flock because discussion with one God has the sense
of prayer about it, if the scribe is clever. Discussion with
three Gods . . . you can well imagine how that goes over
in the world of the stubborn creatures.

Living among them is a rather long night for this soul,
and they serve no better drink than tea. Small wonder,
damned small wonder I prefer silence and solitude to discussion with The Three for recess from the stubborn creatures. The creatures have a special tea for anyone among
them who hears, not to mention *listens*. Voices. We female
scribes, or rather we scribes who are to be born into little
baby female bodies, have our tortured souls full living
among the stubborn creatures. Male scribes live fairly well
uninhibited and blend in well enough to accomplish their
specific missions. Few question male solitude or silence.
Marriage to the creatures is getting a bit tricky for them,
too, though. I don't know how long they can avoid it.

Of the female entrants, I am the one with the most experience; therefore I presume The Holy Three think I am
the only one with the stomach for this mission. The danger for scribes is their susceptibility to creaturehood. Our
numbers are diminishing as rapidly as replacements can
be recruited. The untrained are not yet permitted to de-

scend into the lovely jungle, but things are pressing. And once a scribe succumbs to creaturehood, we never see her for what the creatures call Ever. You see why silence is safer.

Profound regards,
Tere

GARY SOTO

HOME COURSE IN RELIGION

By the time I was eighteen and in junior college
Religion was something like this: The notion
of "project" is an ambiguous substitute for the notion
Of essence of quiddity, and that situation is
An ambiguous substitute for the notion of an
Objective condition resulting from the causes
And natures interacting in the world. That was
The first sentence in a really long book.
I figured that the second sentence had
To be more difficult, and the third almost impossible,
On and on. The back of the book had impressive
Things to say. The author, a French scholar,
Got the Pope to say a few words, and one cardinal
I had heard about remarked, Celebrated thought.
Best Sellers said, It ought to be read by anyone
Who has had a formal or home-study course in metaphysics . . .
I read a chapter, then played basketball to get air
Back into my brain so I wouldn't feel so sleepy,
I returned home, sweaty in every hole,
And picked up a book that sounded like this:
Costly grace confronts us as a gracious call.
To follow Jesus, it comes as a word of
Forgiveness to the broken spirit
And the contrite heart. This was clearer,
But after ten pages my mind jumped to a fact
I had read in the newspaper: Experts on dinosaurs,

Having measured resonating chambers of skulls,
Claim that some of those big beasts groaned tones
Like the tones of French horns. That night
My brother and I, and our two roommates, ate Top Ramen.
After dinner we tape recorded our thoughts
About Nixon, who was in a lot of trouble with Watergate.
We played it back and laughed for a long time
Because none of us understood what the other was saying.
Some of it sounded like this: He won't admit anything about
The submarines or the money. That's all he cares about it.
People with big cars don't know how much it hurts.
Furthermore, if you realize the predicament
Then what's there to say, hmm?
In bed I read four pages about a mystic,
Who lived a common life until lightning struck
Her shoulder, then she began to talk in weird
Ways and no longer reached people with her thoughts.
The next morning I ate cereal
In my Top Ramen bowl. During P.E.
I understood more about life than with the help
Of a book. My karate instructor said,
Pain doesn't exist. Do you see
Pain when you get hit? Pain is something
Of the mind, and the mind is the spiritual nature
That follows your body. Then he matched us
By height and rank, and for twenty minutes
Let us kick and punch one another really hard.
By the time I got back to the apartment I thought
My instructor was wrong. With my one good eye
I could see the pain: red welts on my chest,
And two on my back from running away.
The Bible was much clearer. Jesus said,
O Faithless and perverse generation, how long
Am I to be with you and bear with you? Bring

Your son here. Then I started on my roommate's book
About the Zen Master Xu Yun and was curious how
He could go three years eating only grass
And pine needles. I asked that about myself,
Seeing that I was living on Top Ramen and cold cereal
And oranges that rolled our way when we weren't looking.
That night my girlfriend came
Over with a large jar of peanut butter,
A present that we tried on our last three crackers.
After she left I prayed in my bedroom,
Then crossed myself so that my fingertips
Pushed into my flesh. I then started *The Problem of Evil*,
Which was clearer than my previous readings
Except when I ran into passages like this:
Oderunt peccare mali formidine poenae, oderunt peccare
Boni virtutis amore. I read nine pages
Before I fell asleep, and the next morning
While I ate cereal from my Top Ramen bowl,
I read a paragraph that began, Animal suffering?
Their rate of production demands the existence
Of carnivorousness. But they are not dissatisfied
With life. They do not realize that they
Are suffering. They simply suffer.
In anthropology, I learned about the Papuan people.
In geography, we discussed pumice.
I took notes but mostly watched the teacher,
Sweat stinking up his eyebrows.
My mom called that night,
And I told her that Rick and I were three years short
Of earning good money. She said that as long
As we didn't go to prison she would be
Proud of us. Prison wasn't what I was thinking,
And God knows what I was thinking
When I picked up the book, *What is Man?*

I had to keep looking at the cover to remind me
What I was reading. My girlfriend came
Over and we sat on the couch. Her blouse held a lot
Of shadows, and one was my hand. I liked
That very much, and liked how her mouth fit mine.
She said that she was lonely
When I wasn't around. I said that people feel
Like that because they don't know themselves.
When I placed my hand on her thigh, she opened her legs
Just a little, warmth that was a spooky liquid
When one of my biggest fingers crawled in.
She pushed me away, lipstick overrunning her mouth,
Her hair like the hair you wear when
You wake up from a hard sleep. After she left,
I read in the Bible
About Jesus touching each of his four wounds—
Thomas was not around when Jesus walked through the wall.
I began to feel shamed because my left hand
Turning the pages was the hand that had snapped
Her panties closed. I got up from the couch
And washed that hand, stinky trout that I took to bed.
It was then, on a night of
More Top Ramen and a cat-and-dog storm,
That I realized I might be in the wrong line of belief.

A SUNDAY

That the flesh should go on now seems to matter.
And goodness in the meantime. I'm trying
To be like others in the Church. Katie
Says it's possible, even at this corner,
Leavenworth and Bush, drab men in three sweaters,

Bum on his beat between a boarded-up grocery
And hell. The poor guy has had it. We walk by,
Katie first, then me, and we're all glances.
Maybe that helps, sympathy at a distance.
I know two prayers almost by heart.
Money would help, too, but I feel odd
Floating down a dollar. Katie would see me,
Think, It doesn't help. She would be right
Of course, and all day I would think a dollar
Doesn't help. Two dollars, three,
Three and some change.
We're cold enough to walk by.
At Katie's apartment we need two keys
To get in. We shudder, undo our coats,
And warm our hands with coffee.
We play backgammon, listen to music,
And butter bagels—sesame seeds on all fingers.
The grapes are old, and we throw them away.
She's showing me a photograph of herself,
Then nineteen and with long hair,
When the phone rings—it's her recently married sister.
She's fine, I gather from their talk.
She's bought a new coat, placements,
Exchanged a lamp for a clock radio. Roger,
Her husband, bought her slippers, and sold the boat.
Katie is happy. The lines around her mouth
Deepen as she talks. More lines
On her forehead when she laughs.
She hangs up and says it was her sister
And her sister says Hi.

I like Katie. There's not much to say
Between us. We play backgammon
And neither of us minds losing.
We smile at our losses

And stare out the windows, five flights up
Where pigeons huddle under the shadow-dark eaves.
At this height people don't mind
Being looked at. The shades are up,
The kitchens yellow with light.
The Chinese man in his undershirt is at the stove
Now at the refrigerator, now at the stove.
The woman directly across from us
Is watching television. Light
Like someone shuffling cards. People
Come and go in their pajamas and purple robes.
Katie and I stare out the window.
Sundays are quiet here. She asks
If I would like tea and stupidly I ask,
What kind of tea? I mean to say that I can't take
Caffeine in the afternoon. It keeps me awake.
As she puts on a pot, I thumb through a magazine:
Life seems more real in pictures, and happier.
I want to ask about God, but don't know how.
Katie doesn't know how either. A small, thin cross
Hides behind her top button, sparkles sometimes
When she turns or bends to slip into a shoe.
God troubles me with the same questions.
I want very badly to know how to talk about Christ.
Others seem to know. Katie's friends can run
A finger through the Bible and each chapter,
Some verses. The pot of water comes to a boil.
We lean against the countertop in the kitchen.
God is someone who is with you,
Like now, she says.

The small hours of Sunday gather in the shadows.
I leave Katie, who's running water
In the bathroom sink. You can't see,
She says, and closes the door behind her.

You're married and should know better.
That's true. I think about this as I drive home.
I've been married twelve years, nearly thirteen,
And running water in the bathroom sink
Is a womanly thing. Pantyhose
Drip in the shower, Bras drip, too,
But slower, large drops from secret niches.
When I pull into the driveway,
My wife is watering the begonias.
I take the hose from her hand and drink,
Then pat her hip and say I'm home,
I'm almost hungry. She asks me how mass was.
I say fine. The priest was looking at me
When he spoke about sin. She raises her eyebrows
And says, He knows his parish.
Before we go in she shows me
Where an arbor should go.
I look at the ground and try to find
Something to say. I want my wife to like me.
I look up to a homing pigeon cooing
On the neighbor's fence. We call Mariko,
Our daughter, who comes out of the house
With a book in her hand. That's a homing pigeon,
I point, You see the band on its leg.
We watch the pigeon watch us, and forget about the arbor.
We go inside. Dinner is what we had last night,
Cabbage rolls and a salad. After dinner Mariko
And I play chess, She's nine, smart, and game
Enough to risk a quarter for my five-dollar bet.
Both of us feel cocky, but ten moves into the game.
We're serious. It's different from
Playing with Katie, who wants my company.
Mariko wants my money, a dollar to her dime.
Since I'm a kind fool with dead bishops,

I lose. I shower, and in the shower I sing
A Christian hymn. It's not that I feel that close
To Christ, it's that I like the music.
Most of the words are Holy, Holy, Hallelujah.
And plenty of "forevers."

                    Sunday nights,
With the dishes done and put away,
My wife and I usually dance together. That is,
After we're bathed and in robes,
We dance to oldies on the radio.
My daughter's favorite is Sam Cooke's
"Twisting the Night Away." That's about what
She does, twists until fifteen to nine,
Then it's bed and a few pages from a library book.
But tonight I don't want that music.
I feel OK just sitting on the couch
And reading the travel section in
The newspaper. My daughter
Is speaking Pig Latin. Ello-hay ad-day.
Anks-thay or-fay e-thay ive-fay ollars-day.
It's from a book she's read,
A book that shouldn't have been written
Because she won't be quiet. When she starts
Isten-lay up-way, I shush her and pat my lap.
We read about Annecy in southern France,
A place that looks like France,
Its canals and old buildings and shoppers
Handling fruit at rickety stands. The writer says,
"Thrust in the center of the Thiou,
The exquisite 12th century Palais de L'Isle seemed to
Cut the water like the prow of a dream ship."
The larger the paper, the more the travel writer
Feels for his readers. What man was
Ever so lucky as to throw a newspaper onto

The floor and have his daughter understand?
I bounce her off my knee. Then it's, ood-gay ight-nay,
Which is to say, Goodnight,
But with a hug and a crazy kiss.

Sometimes students will show me panties
When they uncross their legs—pink, white,
Pinkish white. I'm at the blackboard holding
A piece of chalk. This scares me,
The panties I mean, because I want to say
Something smart with the chalk
That "each of them are handsome" is wrong,
That a period goes inside quotation marks.
I want to be nice, of course, and Catholic,
But not so Catholic that I can't at least glance,
Smile inwardly. Once the chalk rolled from my palm
And I didn't dare bend to get it
Because I might see more, or nothing, just black.
The class looked at the chalk
And I looked at the class, said, Let's go home.
That day I was happy. I bought my wife a magazine.
I got myself a southern novel about how nothing fits,
Hats or shoes, and the false teeth of bluish Negroes.
That was months ago. My wife has a new magazine
And I'm reading about a red mountain lion.
It's Sunday, late, and our daughter is in bed,
We're in bed as well. Two moths
Are beating our yellowish lampshade.
An ant is hiding in the folds of an apricot pit.
I have worn Sunday to its end. I like Katie,
And love my wife and daughter,
And believe a dirty face
Is the same as a washed one to God.
I'm going to be like others in the church
And good in the meantime. I close my eyes,

Breathe in and breathe out, and think
Of all the chalk that has ever slipped from my palm,
Chalk that picks up black when it rolls away.
It won't happen again, or if does, I won't look
To see if it's pink or white, or pinkish white.

DRINKING IN THE SIXTIES

Drinking made you popular at school,
And laughing while you drank
Made you everyone's friends. I notice teachers
Laughed when they carried armfuls of books,
And I began to think that they were drunk.
I noticed Mrs. Tuttle seldom kept her legs together,
Lipstick overrunning her mouth. Coach knew only
So many words, and the dean's hand trembled
When he tried to open doors. Our English teacher
Kept repeating "Noun is a person, place, or thing.
You students are a noun, Fresno is a noun,
Bobbie's chair is a noun." Cheerleaders
Were pretty happy when they were thrown into the air.
Scott and I got a brown quart of beer
And sat in an abandoned house at dusk—
The walls were kicked open to chalk
Where rednecks banged heads.
We kept peering out the broken front window
And saying things like, Fuckin' narcs,
When we heard far away voices. I sucked the old air
Of peeling wallpaper
And swigged beer with one eye on Scott.
I told him about the Chinese boy in the iron lung—
Vest of blood, milky skin of nothing to do.
You can live that way, with a hand mirror

To look around corners.
Scott swigged the quart and said
Some rivers peter out before they reach the sea.
I swigged the quart and said that people
With long hair don't laugh as hard,
Except if they're a woman or a clean-cut hippie.
I walked to the window, cursed, Fuckin' narcs,
And Scott with all his strength bent a wire hanger.
I liked the shape it took, and beat a board
Against the wall, chalky dust smothering the good air.
Scott kicked a greenish orange, dead of all sweetness,
Of rain and the bitter seeds.
I kicked the stove. I pulled a calendar from
The kitchen wall. The couch didn't mean
Much to me. We trashed that already trashed house,
And then we were sorry. Scott's hands
Were black. My armpits flooded with worry and sweat.
I swigged the quart, and slammed it hard
Because nothing is what I got. I thought of school:
Mrs. Tuttle's thighs and the cheerleaders cartwheeling
For a last place team.
The coach was farting softly into his bedsheets
And the dean's hand was on the throat of his stinky dog.
His wife smelled. His house was festering
In the chipped paint that could make a stepfather moan.
Scott kicked the living room walls,
I brought a chair down on another chair.
Outside, we threw ourselves on a grave of leaves,
Groaning that we were having a good time.

ALFRED ARTEAGA

CANTO 12
LETTERS OF COLOR

No existe el amanecer. No existe el atardecer. El sol mismo
  ha muerto.
Sólo quedan las nubes. Absolutas. Verdes.
                        –Juan Felipe Herrera

             each
green eye in a heaven of blue, a fistfull
of understanding
                  –Lorna Dee Cervantes

Verde no eres tú
               –Rosario Castellanos

"Green is most sad.
Germany is this color
and shines
this temperature
always . . . "
        —she writes
me in letters. What
could she mean, these
words this breath, these
proofs of woman
to me?
The letters, of course, I know
are not her:
She is not the green. Yet,

because she writes,
I write too. This is true.

So
I collect green: a rain forest monkey
hides there in the tree, I see it; that whale breathes
a cold and broken green, passes the
California point; one green follows the sad
goodbye before the same old sleep,
I get it; bland pages enfold my (for now
I lay claim) color; and the green
I find forged in cannon and fatigue;
these greens
I gather.

But I do not visit Germany, despite
the joy of aluminum for gold,
I can't. Can her letters contain this?
I hold now, this very instant, in
my own hands, the saddest color,
the most Germanic green. Things I
have gathered with my own hands, things
encased in green, essentially green and
things seemingly green to any eye,
I hold. And
because she breathes,
I breathe too. Or this I lie.

I understand primate refuge in trees,
understand migration again
and again past the whaling town
site of slaughter, offal still I'm sure.
I know all the German glyphs like
lines which crease my hands,
I know them.
Yet letters come to me in breath almost

still, she does not tell me more than sad.
I am left only with weapons,
stupidly useless this second. She
writes. I am left with hands full of dumb
color, hands of useless speech that says no
thing, less.
This woman who writes sad green
colors me painted bird
wings before my eyes.

I have made children, planted trees.
I have killed men. I write these words.
My hands are green, I don't know
what it means.

Coyoacán, el otoño gris

Querido Alfredo—

Triste, verde y alemán fue la letra
desaparecida de mi nombre—ojo—te mando una última
letra: ausente, la tehuana-mexicana; presente, el mexicano-
chicano. Escríbeme en caló, escribo, en color.
—Frida

ANDRÉS RODRÍGUEZ

BANNERS

El monte, 1933

Our men drank water and never smoked
as they sat under the walnut tree,
green branches enfolding them,
green leaves flaming with sunlight.
They came each day as dawn approached,
tense dark men crowding together
and speaking low in the presence
of the morning star. We women
could hear the winds shifting south
over the empty fields.

                            Hours passed.
Our children chewed sticks
like ears of corn, dust-devils
whirled and dissolved in the road.
At noon the sheriffs passed
in steaming black cars.
Nothing looked changed: the same
huddled shacks below the sun,
a yellow dog rising from a gully,
dungarees on a sagging clothesline.
So they passed on, riding out
the horizon as our singers
plucked a noisy chord.

                      When they emerged
stiff, morose, the evening rattle

had already begun in the trees.
Tomorrow we'll march to the fields, they said.
We brought them a sip of coffee
cooled by the breath of the night wind
and watched their faces screw up
as they said goodnight and turned homeward
over fields brimming with fruit.

                    * * *

In a week, the strikebreakers came.
Another week and the sheriffs
lured our men into the station
with lies, promises of good work.
And the Mexican consul there
sporting a pencil-stick moustache,
a solemn porky bastard who
sprouted among our dazzled men
calling them "reds." After that,
we kept up the daily pickets
and mass meetings and prayers.

The first time we drove our trucks
through town, forty women maybe,
shouting, making the place a beehive,
raw sunburnt faces stared at us
on every street. That was alright.
But one man, alone, swore at us.
Bracing his hips by the roadside,
hard blue eyes burning right through us,
he wished us bloodied and raped.
I never knew why the town existed,
but now I knew what I felt,
and that was my own heart staring
at itself, blood running not singing.

Returning at twilight, I stared
at the dark fields slipping past us,
the air hot and always doubled,
smell of young berries rotting . . .
Now I could no longer find hope
because we buried three small children
and put the sticks they chewed
upon that ground, one on each grave,
there in the summer harvest light.

* * *

I can still see those nameless stars
poking through the roof slats at night,
green and blue and plum-colored stars.
Eyes shut, I watched them holding still
while I rolled past them on a wave
as if the whole night were an ocean sea.
I never dreamed of food. That night
I woke at the sound of a small
tapping on the roof, the room cool
spread out around me like a wood.
My husband slept, his fine tangled head
on my arm, mouthing words that have
always stayed with me: *ya 'cabaron todo,*
the sticks an' all.
                    The hour comes back
         in the dust thick with panicked men.
Harsh cries sang out from the workers
throwing their heads behind them,
a lightning flash through yellow clouds.
Three were blasted, rolling into
a ditch where they lay face down
licking the mossy earth. Some of us
were pulled away screaming, Murderers!

Brothers! Then we scattered
like a nightmare leaves over the valley.
In a windless orchard we began to cry.

FIRE AND WATER

There was a fire once when they lived together
in the old house. He had cleaned the stove
with kerosene, then turned the burner on.
He would have been killed but for something
that loves a fool. My screaming uncle
ran through every room, *Quick, water!*
Grandfather, helpless and gentle in his wheelchair
laughed at uncle, *¿Pos cómo? ¡No puedo!*
He laughed so hard (he later told me)
that he almost found the strength to walk again.
That was years ago. I remember them now:
Grandfather, toothless, almost ninety,
laughing with all his years at uncle,
gaunt and shriveled and wild with cancer,
looking everywhere, nowhere, for water.
Water would have drowned the flames
and what they needed was fire—
fire for old broken railyard bones,
fire for diseased blackened packinghouse bones.
Sometime later, after uncle had died,
grandfather heard a voice one night
repeating slowly from the withered milpa.
A child? His dead wife calling?
He knew better than to answer the sound
of water rushing around the trees.

TO MY MOTHER

The new year's about to fall,
and all through the neighborhood
it's summer in winter.
The air shines all around.
The maples look studded.
Oh that they might bloom,
Bloom and be the news of life in death
if these final merciful days
could stretch on, undiminished.

We sit the same on the porch
in silence, watching children
fly along the street
trailing Christmas wrappings.
Your eyes, watery and almost blue,
follow them toward your future
beyond the sun-glazed street, the trees,
the sea so far beyond our porch.

Seven winters have sucked your life,
now a suffering thing.
I'd give you mine, mother,
but while you suffer I'm dying to myself,
the child you'll leave behind,
his best hope unmade or betrayed
a second time. The years
darken and fall in you.

Or will my heart be renewed?
You'll leave behind this question, too,
and one of your gestures,
as now you turn toward me, smiling,
and wave at the boys and girls
running into the light,

your arm a splint of palm
wrapped in gauze. That gesture—
and it's one I've never seen,
the turn and look, too, undreamed of—
makes me wish to match the spirit
by which you call to those children
aglow like blossoms beyond the bare trees.

SANDRA CISNEROS

Divine Providence

Why is Alma Alvarado crying? Until today she could wake
to her Mama calling *Alma, Alma,* very gently, the way her
Mama does—*So as to give the soul time to fly back from the
dreams.* The sky was blue and smelled of fresh bread and
oatmeal. The navy blue uniform with the detachable collar
and cuffs waited patiently on its hanger same as always. She
would save a spear of the breakfast papaya for the parrot in
the garden of la Señora Cuca, walk to school with her leather
school satchel on her back, sing the Himno Nacional in a
loud patriotic voice, color a map of the república, eat a ham-
and-cheese torta for lunch, and on the way home buy a bag
of Japanese peanuts from the man with one fat foot and the
other skinny, throw her satchel in the air and catch it, play in
the courtyard—*but not beyond!*—climb the spiral staircase
to the rooftop—clink, clang, clang—peer into the rooftop
room that once belonged to la Luz María before the Abuela
ran her off for stealing a half kilo of butter, tease the mean
dog El Lobo who likes to bark from the roof at anyone who
walks down their street, eat a tangerine and toss the peels
over the wall to the neighbor's chickens, guess how many
shards of glass were cemented on the wall ledge to keep out
the thieves, stare at the volcanoes that once were people but
are now simply volcanoes, read a *Familia Burrón* comic book
and be read to, wash her feet before going to sleep, have
her Mama sing—*Sleep, my little girl, sleep, rrrruuu-rrruuu,
rrruuu-rrruuu, rrrruuu-rrruuu*—all in Spanish which sounds
sweet.

But this afternoon her Mama was busy washing clothes by
hand on the scrub-board sink with a tin bowl of water and a
coffee can of detergent, wedding ring sitting plainly beside the
straw brush, a ring pretty to look through with its rainbow
stone and gold band thick and heavy, the kind of ring a girl
like Alma likes to wear on her own hand to pretend *she* is the
mother, because today her Mama had said yes, finally yes,
while wiping a strand of hair from her face, *yes*, without
looking up, *just leave me be*, pretending she didn't hear the
parrot cries of the Papa's mama, *Just go see what it is your
Abuela wants this time*, the Mama will say, and Alma will
have to go up to the Abuela's room with its scent of candles
and moth balls and overripe fruit, because the Abuela has
fallen into the habit of hiding food under her pillow—*In this
house they never feed me!*—forgetting she already ate an hour
before, will hide hard knobs of bread, or a half tortilla, or
a black banana, or those cookies called fatties that crumble
into a paste and taste like smoke, the ones they fry on grid-
dles in front of the church and wrap in papel de china, all
under the embroidered pillow thinking no one the wiser when
all along a string of brown ants always gives her away, because the Mama can no longer climb up and down the stairs
anymore in her condition since the baby they will name
Reynaldo is asleep inside her Mama's belly, the child her
Mama hopes will anchor her Papa home nights and mend the
marriage like the neighborlady Doña Eufemia Delgado Ruíz
advised.

But now the ring is gone, gone, *I swear I don't know how,
Mama, I swear it was on my hand when I reached to flush
the toilet like so*, and if Señor Meléndez the plumber can't bring
it back, Mama will have her baby right now from so much
nerves and crying, while the Abuela is screaming in her mad
parrot voice for her supper, the Papa on the telephone, and
the Mama lying down with a cold washcloth on her forehead,
and the water swirled, Mama, swirled without a nose or tail
when the Mama's ring leapt from her hand and disappeared

with two little sausages of caca, and now there is no way to
bring the ring back except by pumping furiously this useless
plunger, though perhaps the ring is floating through the sew-
ers of Mexico City by now, and into the muddy canals of
Xochimilco where a plump woman in a green satin cocktail
dress is trailing a pink hand from a flowered chalupa named
Perlita, beyond the floating gardens and beneath the ruins of
an abandoned city where an eagle once perched on a cactus
and bit a serpent, and has swooped and tumbled and somer-
saulted into the eddies and spirals of the Gulf of Mexico waters that are as warm and salty as tears, while, no doubt,
little and big sharks are nibbling on a ragged piece of seaweed
the moment the ring settles finally on the bottom with a
soundless poof of sand.

And it will be just as his mother predicted long ago for going
against her better judgment and marrying a girl beneath his
station in life. Unless the ring comes back like the neighbor
lady Doña Eufemia Delgado Ruíz advised, the marriage will
be finished regardless how many candles are lit, or promises
made, or supplications to Saint Anthony recited, Ave María,
Padre Nuestro, world without end, amen. Why is Alma Alvarado crying?

RAY GONZÁLEZ

THE ENERGY OF CLAY

1

Of the hands, I say nothing.
The brown dirt embeds itself.
It sparks a dream out of the fingers.
I sink them into the moisture
and fall off the cliff
to find my father
at the bottom of the canyon,
digging with his bare hands,
molding clay figures of his daughters,
my mother, our house,
even as the rain
washes it all away
and covers him with the gray mud
of the one who can create anything.

2

Beyond the color of the sticky mud,
I gain wisdom to smear it
across my forehead,
paint my face as the son who slept
in the soil to find
the wanderings of the blood,
the gloves of mud that crack
into the palms we will follow
when we shape our first sculpture,
wake from the dream of hair and dirt

to go cut a fresh slab of clay
out of the heart of
the dry statue of my father.

3

In the caked daydream,
too many whispers that
the world will end in clay.
In the water splashed on the face,
then on the mound of clay—
a puddle, a mess, a reflection,
hands on a sculpture of a world
that gives up its rocks,
its adobe walls,
that wets the family down
so they can dissolve back to clay.

4

My mother said, "If you drink from the clay jar,
you can taste the desert."
She would look for tiny grains of dirt,
chips of the inner jar that fell in the water.
"If you crunch the dirt in your teeth,
you can taste the earth."
We drank from the jar,
inhaled the dark smell
of the cold water like
the odor of an undiscovered cave
somewhere beyond our house,
an underground spring
we dared to dig up,
the earthy taste of the jar
filling us with the need
to go down deeper,

to settle into the cave
like we had no choice—
our thirst meant we were
fated to go under,
never to look up at the sky,
always down to the ground
where the water jars sprang
like brown wombs of the mothers
quenching our thirst,
giving us our first taste of clay.

5

I come up and roll the dirt,
praise the new green color of clay
for being pure, but sharper
and hotter than the cactus
I tried to construct out
of the spreading clay.
I pound the soil like
the last traveler afraid water
from clay will not save him.

I push my palms together.
The face of the desert emerges
from my oozing hands.
The face of my father falls
into the cactus.
The faces of the rocks melt
into more clay.
The face of the sweetness of earth
takes shape from the clay ruins.
Then, the face of the clay-maker
turns green and dries into
the face of the dirt-dreamer.
And, the dirt-dreamer lifts

the clay into the face
of the clay jar that overflows with water.

6

Of the family, I know little.
They left to churn the mud
into a life they could accept.
Of my father, he lives in two worlds—
land of the canyon dweller,
and the hole of the clay,
territory he can never inhabit
because his adobe houses were
built from harder ground,
a mixture of the bitter cottonwood
and the pure acid of the thorn,
formed with the isolation
of the walls where all fathers,
in their son's clay dreams,
go and lie down to forget.

7

The sun bakes the clay without ovens,
gains the upper shadow
on the hard mud,
set into features by my fingers.
The sun goes down,
out of the way
of the clay-shaper who dreams alone
and digs in a new canyon
where the clay comes up
black and alive,
perfect for the fingers
where moisture seeps and obeys
the dreams of the masked hands.

THE BLUE SNAKE

I stand in the reptile house,
look for the blue snake that
calls me to join it on display,
amuse ourselves by spitting at
strangers who love snakes.

I walk over the tiled passageway
in search of the diamondback
I hacked as a boy, slicing it
with the shovel I always possessed,
watched it become the blue snake
in a desert where every bug,
lizard and fly I ever killed
changed color before my eyes.

I curl up the tree, wait to be fed,
too wise to hunt the frog,
preferring the rat in the cage,
the meal coming to me,
afraid I will miss it if I move
too deeply into the trees.

I pass the locked door into the glass
where the blue snake waits hungry,
yet fed, alive but unseen,
still not found by me.

I leave after searching each stall,
but the boa and copperhead have a long way
to go before turning blue, neither one
knowing me when I killed blue lightning
to prevent a storm of open flesh,
drove metal through muscled ground
in search of blood that never came,

my wonder over the clean pieces
sending the snake on its way
before I could enter the glass,
find the hidden blue eyes sparkling
off the wire where the rattle
misses a beat for me.

HOMAGE TO LUCIAN BLAGA

1. Brief Beginning

> *Be glad on the blossom and understand—*
> *We don't have to know now who brings and spreads fire.*
>   *Lucian Blaga*

We know the flame kisses
what we believed in,

but we take the mystery of invasion
against the great burning,

find a way to guess what
presence breathes fire,

which companion
shares water.

We hold the match to the finger
and paint a change of skin upon ourselves

as punishment for not knowing
when to strike,

not accepting this self-branding is not
the way to learn the language of smoke.

2. Heaven and Earth

Astir under the trees God makes himself
smaller to give the red mushrooms
room to grow under his bark.   *L.B.*

He lies down to fill
the earth with poison.
He is under the leaves
exciting the ground to stand erect,

red mushrooms pushing through
to spit at the world like
tiny demons escaping the embrace
of a god they never thought would come down.

3. Fate

In sleep my blood draws me back
into my parents like a wave
                    L.B.

Entering their bodies,
I finally see why it happened this way.
I recall the first words
I ever cried, seconds after birth,
their sound an incoherent message
to them to let go,

to let me come out and wait
for the answer from their lips,
so I could grow the way
I should have gone,

so I could make it through this passage
without having to look back
at their hesitation, postponement,
desire, consummation,

without having to relive taking
the wrong turn into the belly of their soul.

4. Asking

*Look, the stars are coming into the world
at the same time as my sorrowful questions.*
                                        L.B.

How far do they travel
before we wish they would explode?
When was the last time we spoke
the same instant a falling star
streaked over our heads?
How much do I have to reveal
without using their light?

Who decided stars had something
more than their burning energy?
Why do we continue to overlook the comet?
Where do they go after we understand?

How can we trust the universe
when it expands without us?
Why do we insist on looking up?
What does sorrow have to do with
that oncoming mass of light?

5. Without Regret

*How humbly bends the arrogant forehead
of yesterday's ecstasy*   L.B.

Last night, we gave it everything
and clutched each other
so we couldn't stop to catch our breath,
or follow each other to
the peak of our breasts.

We kept at it all night and hurried
through the signs of love
to reach the morning as one body,
giving up identity to bow before
ecstasy, allow the naked body
to invent a new way of finding out,
a flesh-driven need to escape from desire
so we could face the world that demanded
we fall before our creator,
the still, moist ground that insists
on punishing the lovers who rolled
and crawled out of its reach.

6. Back

I stand turned toward my country—
return is a dream I cannot wake from.
                                    L.B.

I am constantly returning,
going back across the border
where the river rose and fell,
dried before me like a dream
of crossing a great canyon that
opened toward the frontier,

my nameless country where
I want to settle as the man
who made it here,
got this far by turning my back
on mountains of a lost child.

I cannot wake from this dream
of coming back to see
if the desert rains cracked
everything away,
to revisit old adobe where I found

answers cut into the walls like
a map carved by those who
preceded me into the dream,

the point where they fell
into the river,
years before it dried up,
fell into the deep water
finding themselves at home,
about to wake up.

FRANCISCO X. ALARCÓN

LAMENTARIO	LAMENTARY
es triste	how sad
ser vaso	to be a glass
y nunca	and never
llenarse	be filled
ser puerta	a door
y siempre	and stay
quedarse	always
trancada	locked up
ser cama	a bed
sentirse	that's
mortaja	a deathbed
no lecho	not a nest
es triste	how sad
ser uno	to be oneself
y nunca	and never
sumar dos	add up to two
ser ave	a bird
sin nido	without a nest
ser santo	a saint
sin vela	without a candle
ser solo	to be alone
y vivir	and live
soñando	dreaming
abrazos	embraces

POBRES POETAS

a Miguel Angel Flores

por las calles
rondan poetas
como pajaritos
caídos del nido

dan con los postes
del alumbrado
que de pronto
les salen al paso

ceremoniosos
les piden permiso
a las bancas vacías
de los parques

nadie sabe
ni ellos mismos
por qué les brotan
en los hombros alas

un día quizá usen
por fin esa llave
que desde siempre
traen en el bosillo

POOR POETS

to Miguel Angel Flores

poets walk aimlessly
on the streets
like chicks fallen
from their nest

they bump into
light posts
that suddenly
cross their path

ceremoniously
they ask permission
from empty benches
in the parks

nobody knows
not even themselves
why wings sprout
from their shoulders

maybe one day finally
they'll use that key
they always carry
inside a pocket

SILENCE

I smell
silence
everywhere

clean
nice homes
smell

banks
smell
so do malls

no deodorant
odorizer
or perfume

can put away
this stink
of silence

WE ARE TREES

our roots
network

with the roots
of other trees

our branches
grow

with desire
of touching

other branches

ISLA MUJERES

¿por qué
no entrar
a cualquier
casa de
pescador
y decir:
"ya llegué"
una vez
sentados
a nuestras
anchas
suspirar:
"es una larga
historia . . . "

why not
just go
into any
fisherman's
house
and say:
"I'm home"
and once
seated
at our
ease
sigh:
"it's a long
story . . . "

EXTRANJERO

hoy
lo compruebo
lo padezco:

dondequiera
extranjero
soy

FOREIGNER

today
it's real
and hurts:

I am
a foreigner
everywhere

IVÁN ARGÜELLES

THESE THINGS

the dark which takes all these things
and makes them indiscriminate as days
one after the other galloping in blind light
through war jungle or labyrinthine thought
these things painted white or red and sharp
or oblong as memory going down the shaft
partnership of shape and resonance aloft
battered in the sudden whim of bad weather
clouds numbered in yards of tufted dream
like hair unruly or the violent occasion of blood
in the advantage of ether climbing the stairs
celestial the pattern of flight into the deep
which darkness obliterates removing from sight
childhood landscapes these things blunted stiff
in the winter of a grandmother's starched eye
beyond sleep or the cataclysms of pre-speech
in the cliff-signs of those who have "seen"
but were never able to articulate the experience
dumbfounded turning like animals on the floor
to generate power for some alien purpose
these things with their single vowel O
distracted by the sex of origins and decay
mouths filled with dry turf a spear in the back
horses rattling emptied chariots over spine
the liturgical voice empowered like an azure wedge
slammed into the insane air of dust and sand
like hematite flashing their eyes in agony

perceiving a depth in the heaven of accident
grammar of wounds splintered in bilabial fear
which the dark taking all these things does
to fusion of tongue to dirt as a new matter
crowned by the gold of Shekinah's invisible waist
and the space of the page it takes to describe it
or walls fiercely erected overnight above the torso
& rivers forked like diphthongs in a quotation
"who am I in this mass of unspecified particulars?"
unfinished shrine where horse is sacrificed
and the seed of generations spilt in vain
or the stone knife and the loaded dice of greed
into the channel strewn where growing muddy
the diaphanous appearance of youth rusts
a lotus broken in its spirit like a last tooth
these things absconded from the wheel of chance
elaborated for a brief blazing instant
between the ears of a splendid but nameless deity
these things in the cadaver's faint echo
a shattered piano revenged by fate's window
these things when silence impends its paragraph
like hands directed to grope in the groin of nothing
these things an extinct wind in unplowed pleasure
the last the lost unwinding from the skein
whose rain a man's fall litters in the dark

CURRICULUM VITAE

going crazy for the first time
during Xerox process of decades
great honor to be a foreigner
on one's knees knocked by the muse

moving as a satellite of light
through various gravid conditions
father like a knife of thought
mother folded inside the white album
history of ideas in a green syllabus
intended for the hammerklavier lesson
notations inside a pentagram
indicating a future in spanish education
dividing attention between marriage
and breath insulating the person
from the world's insidious microphones
none of the familiar fabric remains
then a song without an agenda
the particulars of a prussian music
as if to initiate a conversation
with the many dead philosophers
communing on labels for the gods
in celestial dialogue but unconscious
purchase a woman for natural reasons
gnostic intercourse & tantra asana
experimenting with chemical substances
disarranging the art history industry
yesterday yawning into the big time
a cage with alternate hospitals
and a son hit by unexpected seizures
in course of time denying the course
causality and the tractatus
interrupted monologues with Nostalgia
fortune to write about writing
in curves planting one's isolation
clean up in the evenings with reckless sleep
sometimes dreading the next perception
"I am the stranger driven from/
the land of Memory and Beauty"

a task to recall the higher numbers
hushed in the oracular withdrawal
political associations of sexual contact
shaping the goddess' buttocks
out of pure air the ethereal one
the slant of danger in a library
shoplifting minor thoughts from a folio
or sequencing the cultural symbols
as if to classify chemical dissolutions
that burn into the ancient history books
that a lecture disturbs the myth
gathering all the waters in a square
defining the mile left to go
but home? the radical for "ear"
listening intently for the wheels
to crunch over the night gravel
to understand which are the limits
in the failing of all aspirations

ENRIQUE BERUMEN

CORNER

nobody knows
what I carry:

nights with days
spreading of lips
oven-heated embraces
noisy wells lying
          on a deserted Chesapeake Bay
cloudy windows
          with stains of hasty breath

at the edge
of a broken
little corner

NELSON

por 27 y pico de años:
tu carne encerrada
y tu presencia
papable
volando
por cielos extranjeros

hasta el gran día
cuando levantabas tu puño
como lo hacías antes

pero hoy tu grito
resonaba más:
poder popular

portabas
cara de boxeador
peleador callejero
sobreviviente
de infinito rounds:
ganchos
cabezazos
jabs
codazos
golpes bajo la cintura

pero al sonar
la campana
la victoria te bañaba
mientras el cuadrilátero del mundo
te levantaba
alto
elevándote
tan alto
que no se distinguía
donde empezaba
o terminaba
el cielo

tan inmenso
como tu sonrisa

NELSON

for 27 years
incarcerated
your presence
palpable
flying
throughout foreign skies

until the great day
when you raised your fist
as you had done before
but
today your cry
was louder than ever:
people's power

you wore
a boxer's face
street fighter
survivor
of infinite rounds:
hooks
head butts
jabs
elbowing
blows below the belt

but
when the bell sounded
victory soaked you
while the world ring
lifted you
high
lifting you so high
that it was difficult

to tell where the sky
began or ended

the sky,
immense

just like your smile

NORMA CANTÚ

Se me enchina el cuerpo al oír tu cuento . . .

how the day after graduating as valedictorian from the high
school in the Rio Grande Valley you helped your family board
up the door and windows of the frame house and pack the old
pick-up truck to make your annual trek north. After three
days on the road arriving at the turkey farm and being led to
your quarters. The family, tired, looks to you. "What's this?"
you ask, for you, the favored son, speak English; you can
communicate with the bosses.

"This is where you're gonna live."

Perplexed you say, "But it looks like a chicken coop."

"It is, but it's not good enough for the chickens," the Anglo
responds with a sneer.

And you take it, and you suffer as your mother and your
sisters make the best with the chicken coop. They hang curtains and sweep the floor and burn candles to the Vírgen.

Then the work, arduous and demeaning, begins. Working
night shifts after long days . . . plucking feathers, forcibly
breeding the toms and the hens, and your Dad ages from day
to day before your very eyes.

Until one day you've been working hard, and you look for
your Dad, and barely see his head in one of the buried barrels
full of feathers, working away. Suddenly he's gone, and you
think you're imagining things; how could he disappear? and
you remove your gloves and risk the foreman's wrath. You run
to your father; jump in; he is almost smothered by feathers,
and you say, Enough!"

You take control and pack the family off. "No pay for all
your work if you leave."

And you say, "We're leaving." The favored son, who speaks to the bosses, has spoken. And driving the Midwest farm road almost crossing the state line you spy a sign "Labor Relations," and you stop. And, yes, you are owed your wages, and the bosses pay reluctantly. No one had ever done that before. But you read the language of the bosses. You move on with your family, and your father is pleased; your mother beams but is afraid in her heart for her son who speaks the language of the bosses.

Years later a lover will wonder why you refuse to sleep on feather-filled pillows, and you want to tell, to spill your guts, but you can't, you refuse. You hold your words like caged birds.

Memory's wound is too fresh.

And more years later when you tell the story, I cringe and get goosebumps; you tell your story and are healed, but there's still a scar and like an old war wound or surgical scar it hurts when the weather changes or the memory intersects with this time and place.

C. S. FOSTER

NO MATCHES

I watch her from three stools down
her skinny fingers caressing the Camel filter
as she waits with great and fragile dignity
for a light from the gentleman
who fell into the harbor and drowned
on their honeymoon night

and so I will get up and light her cigarette
as I have done many times before
and she will once again manage
to form a feeble smile for me
on lips that are painted into
a grotesque little bow

and she will say to me:
"thank you, young man, you are a gentleman"
(her voice cracking on "GENTLEMAN"
breaking every last heart in the joint)
and she will go back to her martini
and I will go back to my stool

and late that night I will read Cheever
and bask in the warmth
of my sleeping wife's breasts
nuzzled deep into my back
as I die once more for the old widow
with no matches.

MR. & MRS. MCCLUSKEY

McCluskey sits
in his favorite chair
watching Vanna White
parading back and forth
across the 19-inch
color Zenith
and McCluskey
red-eyed, jowly
full-of-gas McCluskey
takes a long, slow pull
from the Burgermeister and
watches the letters turn
one by one
and Vanna
always smiling Vanna
never stumbling Vanna
looking and smiling out
at this fat man
a beer bottle perched
on his enormous
retired chief's belly
as he sits and stares
and remembers a 21-year-old
seaman second class
tanned and lean and
a million miles away
from McCluskey's South Phoenix
air-conditioned mobile home

meanwhile, Mrs. McCluskey
sad-faced and wrinkled and
not so far down the road
drags heroically .

on her Benson & Hedges
puts down her third
bloody mary
gets up and prepares to make
the seven-ten split
and when she misses
Mrs. McCluskey's whiskey laugh
fills up the great, spacious
suburban bowling alley
with the ghost of blond
honey-skinned Miss Honolulu 1939
who just happened to fall in love
with this man who sits back
in an air-conditioned mobile home
farting and watching Vanna White
turning letters.

RAMÓN GARCÍA

LA PIÑATA: A SELF-PORTRAIT

Hanging from a tree,
the tree's own suicidal outgrowth;
I am a fruit, a watermelon slice, a bull,
a toy, a pig, a bird—
I am many forms,
dangerous and childish,
some insane god's creation.
I am filled with small, sweet treasures.

I am alone in my splendor.
The children are gone.
There is no one below me,
nothing but green grasses
sleeping in their death bed of earth.

I exist but for this ritual,
mystic sticks hitting me with consciousness,
my created being breaking,
words falling through the cracks.

FOR FRIDA KAHLO

the green grasses of anguish
grow touching buried gods
under worn-out fields long ago
scorched by visionary suns

the forest echoes absences,
green and brown shadows,
an ocean longs for your final blue silence,
the moon struggles to establish
the mirror of your image

your flesh is the earth,
it feeds only pain,
but your veins run red
flowering on the dark skin of the land,

your blood is spilt in the sands of oblivion,
the gods were blind before you gave them sight,
they thirst in the desert,
you are their oasis.

PAT MORA

THE YOUNG SOR JUANA

I

I'm three and cannot play away my days to suit
my sweet *mamá*, Sleep well, my dolls, for I must run
to school behind my sister's frowns. She knows my secret
wish to stretch, if only I were taller, if only I could
tell *Mamá* why I must go, my words irresistible as roses.

My sister hears my tiptoes, knows her shadow
has my face. I tiptoe on, for I must learn to unknit words
and letters, to knit them new with my own hand.
Like playful morning birds the big girls giggle, at me,
the little tagalong. I hear the grumble of my sister's frown.

I stretch to peek inside, to see the teacher's face,
How it must glow with knowledge. Like the sun
A woman so wise has never tasted cheese. She sees
my eyes and finally seats me near. My stubborn legs
and toes refuse to reach the floor.

At noon I chew my bread. Others eat soft cheese.
I've heard it dulls the wits. I shut my lips to it.
I must confess, when tired, I slowly smell the milky moons,
like *Mamá* savors the aroma of warm roses.
I linger, imagine my teeth sinking into the warm softness.

II

I'm seven and beg to leave my sweet *mama*, to hide
myself inside boys' pants and shirt, to tuck

my long, dark hair inside a cap so I can stride
into large cities, into their classrooms, into ideas crackling
and breathing lightning.

Instead of striding I must hide from frowns,
from dark clouds in the eyes of my *mama*. I hide
in my grandfather's books, sink into the yellowed
pages, richer than cheese. Finally *Mama* releases me
to her sister. I journey to the city. If only I were taller.

III

I'm sixteen and spinning in the glare of Latin
grammar. I cannot look away. Beware, slow wits,
I keep my scissors close, their cold, hard
lips ready to sink into this dark, soft hair,
punish my empty head, unless it learns on time.

I'll set the pace and if I fail, I'll hack and slash
again until I learn. I'll pull and cut, this foolish lushness.
Again I'll feel my hair rain softly on my clothes, gather
in a gleaming puddle at my feet.
My hands are strong, and from within I rule.

HELENA MARÍA VIRAMONTES

Tears on My Pillow

Mama Maria learned me about La llorona. La llorona is the one who doing all the crying I've been hearing all this time with no one to tell me who it was til Mama Maria. She told me La llorona's this mama, see, who killed her kids. Something like that. How does it goes? Something like there's this girl and some soldiers take her husband away and she goes to the jail to look for him, asses why these soldiers took him. And she gots I don't member how many kids all crying cause their daddy's gone, you know. And the soldier being mean and stupid and the devil inside him (but that's okay cause God knows everything says Mama Maria), he points a gun to her head and says "I gonna kill you." But she looks at him and says "Do me the favor." That's like something Arlene would say, you know. But the girl she don't know when to stop. "You kill everything so go ahead and kill me," she tells the soldier, "but first kill my kids cause I don't want 'em hungry and sick and lone without no ama or apa or TV." So the devil says "okay," and shoots all the kids, bang, bang bang. But you know what? He don't kill her. Cold shot, huh? She goes coocoo and escapes from the nut house like my Grandpa Ham used to do before he got dug in at Evergreen. And to this day, the girl all dressed up in black like Mama Maria cause she killed her kids and she walks up and down City Terrace with no feet, crying and crying and looking for her kids. For reallies, late in the dark night only.

   You could hear her crying, for reals, I swear. When you hear her crying far away that means she's real close so don't go out at night. She's as close as your bed, so don't sleep with

your feet to the window cause even she can pull you out.
She'll get you, I swear. Ask Mama Maria. She's too old to lie.

Arlene don't believe me either. Not til she's home on a Friday night with nowhere to go but here. She heared it, too,
herself, covered my ears. Ssshhh, my mama Arlene said.
Make it stop, I told her. Make it stop. I wished to God for
Gregorio to come home. He's mean and can kick La llorona's
ass to the moon. Arlene took me to her bed, and I pulled
up my feet real close to her. She smelled like cigarettes and
warm beer and Noxzema cream. Her chichis was soft and
cool under her slip, where I put my head. Please, mama,
make it stop. I asses her to put the TV on real loud, do
something, cause La llorona was crying so crazy, she was
breaking windows.

Ssshh, Arlene said, turning off the light, ssshhh.

* * *

La llorona only comes at night. When it's day, Veronica will
always stay. That's what I say. I don't like Veronica. Not cause
her skin was all scaly and yellow and pusy 'round the elbows
and neck and behind her knees. Not even, cause she's been
hold back a few grades and just gets taller, or the way spit
always dried at the corners of her mouth and turned white.
I'm ascared of her cause her mama died a few months back,
when the hot so hot you could fry your toes on the tar street.
And every time I seen her, I member of its possible for my
mama to die too. And my stomach burns bad to see her, tall
and ugly and bad luck stuck to her like dried pus.

I have to sit next to Veronica on account of both our last
names begin with G., no relation. She smells like pee and no
one talk to her 'cept for Miss Smith, but she don't answer to
nobody, not even Miss Smith. Veronica forgets that her name
begins with V, puts spit on her eraser to erase the T on paper.
Watching her smear the T all greasy black, then seen her
scratching, scratching makes me want to tear out to any-
wheres. But Veronica, she lives close to me too.

Veronica and the brat brothers live 'cross the street from us in City Terrace Flats. Everybody ugly in her family, 'cepting her mama, Lil Mary G. Arlene knew her mama cause they went to Belvedere Jr. High together and hung around at Salas drugstore afterwards. Then they got old.

Once when Arlene and me are in the bra section, First Street Store, cuz' Arlene needs a new bra cause the thing that makes the straps go up and down broke and so her chichis hang down like a cow's she told Pancha, Veronica came up with Lil Mary G. For the first time, I seen Veronica's mama up front. She was short, kinda lumpy in a Arlene sorta way, which even made Veronica look more longer and ropey with knots for hands. Arlene said:

"Hey Lil Mary G! Member when we had to wear these, member?" Meaning Arlene picked up this kinda crippled bra for beginner chichis to show her. Lil Mary G. don't look like she even related to Veronica. I'm thinking about how someone so purty could have someone so ugly for a kid. She had glued, black Maybelline falsie lashes, black liner on top and at the bottom of her eyes, raccoon style. And she got's these gray eyes like rain clouds. Ain't never seen color in eyes like that before. She wore her hair beehive teased, looked bitch'n cause you couldn't even see the bobby pins. But even, I seen the way Veronica looked at me staring at her mama, the way I check her out her skin so tissuey and Veronica gets all proud at her mama.

"Ain't buying this for Veronica," said Lil Mary G. and grabbed Veronica's chichis and Veronica gets all bare-assed, unknots her hands and flapped Lil Mary G. chichis back, kinda laughing, kinda pushed out of shape. "Its for me," and Arlene and Veronica's mama had a good laugh between the rows of boxes with them bra girls pushing out their starched up tits, thinking they all look Hot. No one 'cepting me don't even pay no attention to the way Veronica always scratching, scratching her arm, behind her legs or the spit all white on her mouth even in the bra section at the First Street Store.

* * *

Arlene was in the kitchen. Got her rollers the size of candles all waxed stiff with Deb gel. She looked to be a shadow at the kitchen window, sitting in the dark, and for a snap of a minute, cause maybe I woke up all sleepy head, I think it's a ghost. Mama? but she don't answer me, just the radio real low, a man singing Arlene's favorite song. You don't member me, but I member you, was not so long ago, you broke my heart in two—I peek over her to see what she's looking at.

"Crying shame" was all I heard, shaking her head like she does when Grandpa escaped and no one ever knowed where he was. The peoples down below all grouping next to Lil Mary G.'s house, the ambulance doors scream open and the bed rolls out like a tongue. I seen a plastic bag and lots of tubes, red period spots on white sheets, the tongue swallowed up by the ambulance mouth. I don't see Veronica nowheres, and I stick my head out to look for her but Arlene grabbed me back in real hard, like she's piss at me for something. "I hope they blow his fucking dick off," she tells no one.

* * *

Veronica don't talk to no one, and purty soon no one talk to her. She just wants to be left alone til everybody forgets she's around. I think that's what it is. Then she can disappear like Lil Mary G. without no one paying no attention. You don't need bras or nuthin' when you just air.

But to me, she just gets taller and rashier and her scratching sounds louder, like someone always rubbing sandpaper together. For reals.

Miss Smith yelled to me in a voice coming from a deep cave, "Ofelia, answer my question!" cause she been calling me and who cares, I don't know the answer anyways and I said "I dunno the answer anyways" and the bell rings. I ain't allowed to stay after school and play with Willy on account of he bit me like a dog, and Arlene and Tia Olivia had a fight, sos I ain't allowed to go to Tia's house either and I dunno where my brother Gregorio is sos I guess I just go straight home, put the TV on loud or something.

When the door opens and its Arlene, my stomach burns stop. Her face make-up is all shiny sweat. Last week, me and Arlene and Pancha, who can drive a pick-up truck, go to where Arlene works on account of I might get this job there pulling pant pockets inside out and getting money for it. Pancha can't find no parking so its just me and Arlene that goes into this big room with pipe guts for ceilings and no windows. All these sewing machines buzzing, buzzing, eating up big balls of string about big as my head spinning dizzy and so much dust flying 'round, makes it hard to breathe where Arlene works. Even I sneeze to no God bless yous. Nobody even to look up to say hello, not even Mr. Goldman who's so red he's pink 'n' says I'm too young anyways. Arlene said everyone at the machines ascare to go pee cause when you come back, might some other girl be in your place and no more job for you. Sos she got to hold her piss—'til my pussy 'bout to pop—she said to Pancha at the Kress lunch counter and I heard.

"Turn off the TV," she always says before hello. "Get me some aspirins." And I does both. I know it takes a long time for the buzzing of the machines in your head to stop. I know it after last week. Arlene kicks off her tennies, goes straight for the couch. The gummy black mascara lashes close like venetian blinds, puts her arm over her forehead, asses me, "Where's Spider?"

"I dunno."

"Was he home?"

"I dunno."

"Did he go to school?"

"I dunno." And in a snap of a minute, she's asleep.

Sos not to wake her, I go to the kitchen, look out the window for Gregorio. I see Veronica across the street, sitting on the porch, licking her lips, and I act like I don't see nuthin'. She act like she don't see nuthin' either.

* * *

"What the fuck's wrong?" Arlene yells, running into the bath-room, her hair wrapped in a towel like a vanilla Foster Freeze ice cream. "Well?" She's pissed, unwraps her towel, bows to rewrap it.

"Oh," I says, wiping my nose with the back of my hand, feeling stupid. "It's nuthin' ama. I just thought you. . . . "

"Cheezes, mi'ja. Don't do me that again, sabes?"

I dunno what to say. One minute I seen her in the tub, next minute I run into the bathroom and stand there and the tub is empty and I only seen the water circling and circling into the drain and I screamed for I dunno why. Ain't nothing worser could happen than for a mama to die, you know. They ain't supposed to. Not even with such a purty name like Lil Mary G.

Just they never say hello and they never say goodbye. Mama Maria never said goodbye, she just left and that's that and no-body to tell me why tio Benny don't live with tia Olivia any more or when is Gregorio gonna come home or if Arlene is fixed up to go dancing at the Paladium tonight. No one to say nuthin'.

Arlene is getting ready in front of the mirror, pulls the top of her hair up, teases it with a brush, brushes it back, forks it high with her comb. I trip out cause she can do this and blow bubble gum at the same time without missin' a beat. Sprays Aqua Net back and forth, back and forth til her hairdo as shiny and hard as candied apples.

See what I mean? They just never say hello and never say goodbye. They just disappear, leaving you alone all ascared with your burns and La llorona hungry for you.

CÉSAR A. GONZÁLEZ-T.

LOS SCHOLARSHIPS I

Le dieron finan$hul age
a mis compadres
y ahora ay me los tiene, muy instruidos
como discos rotos, alborotados:

Que primero la agricultura
y luego que los revolucionarios industriales,
que no sé cuántas.

—In the stillness of myth/en
on the third day marks rose!
me dice mi comadre.

—Cálmese! Slow down, comadre! Le digo.
Y . . . cómo . . . cómo estuvo esa movida?

Luego resulta que todo se 'voluciona
que diga "léctica" a no sé cuántas,
los padrecitos son puro bulchet
y que "your ol-fechund"
. . . así, todo de un jalón,
y why don' you get with it, camarada?

—No se crea de esas carambadas, Comadre
le digo: Sí, todo se pasa,
eso cualquier bruto lo ve,
pero a la larga, como en familia,
tiene que haber alguien que no se alborote,
algún centro, algo que no se despepite,

o si no, no hubiera nada,
todo sería puro desmadre
como una costura deshilvanándose.

—Tiene que haber base, decía mi abuelito.
Si no, como chinga'os vamos adelantar?

—Do you have a shovel, Compadre?

LOS SCHOLARSHIPS II

Why demean "pre-industrial man," Manita?
as though s/he were some pre-Raphaelite Chicanada
with a blush of folk culture?
You confound matter with art,
the verse with the vision inversed
the song and the sound, force with the driven flow
you miss the point of communion with the comida.

There in sight was thought plowing the brow
in the cave in the furrowed silent
space of wonder-widened hearts,
the meta-communion of spirits,
searching for the mean in faith,
in-thought commingled with such scientific measure.
The many-windowed mansions of the spirit

And is not the clamor of lights in
the stillness of a billion nights, always there
daily given, again and again passed round,
maybe once we won't miss the point
of the earthy hitchings of nature's pulse,
in every seasons' coming flow, fall of leaf and wing
flight, brushed in the borne wind,

striated in the color slash in the sway of
the fields there sketched in the constant
lilt and litany lifting the brow to light?
And is not the face drawn finally to "truth
in the heart" again, as it is ever,
in illo tempore?
The many-windowed mansions of the spirit

So now, all rise for the last gospel:
There's just stuff.
And the new inquisitors general
unsheathe their common denominators
to slaughter all innocent magnificats—
all Alphas of nonconformity.
Yet beyond the symmetry of fields lies beauty,
they say, so superlative, unseen
it must be canonized in human assumption.

And the aspiring, untired spirit
flames and flows beside itself, ecstatic.
The star-leaper, exults,
will toward the Omega
The many-windowed mansions of the spirit

JUAN FELIPE HERRERA

BLOWFISH
AN AUTOBIOGRAPHY

> *I cannot miss my way—I breathe again.*
> William Wordsworth

I. Seascape

He loved to leave the house early, roam
through the lonely streets of the city, consider
the weights, hues and figures around him

and in this reverie ride to his secret territory,
the beach—to lose himself once again,
in the translucent, raging of the sea.

He could call on the brothers and sisters
that he never had, speak to that wavy legged boy,
the one he could talk to so easily
on that brilliant shore.

These waters soothed him, caressed his
tiny heart, ringed with scales, hooks
and little fins pulling him deeper,

into the ocean's mad gills where one night
he realized he could see.

II. Depot

I am leaving
the priests behind. Let them count the tears in their frank-
incense; all the possible penance sealed inside the front door

lock. Wind, storm, and songs shall escape from their predes-
tined vaults, inevitably. I served my altar boy years at Guadalupe Church on Kearny Street. Now, I walk the grid at the
mouth of the gutter facing 14th Street. Pool halls, the Flores
family garage and Chinese laundries make this history. This is
my Vale, my shore of Patterdale.

My mother Lucha and my dad Emelio live here too. This is
our depot. Not a house or one of those polished squares where
the eerie emulsion of permanence has taken hold. Not yet.
We love to roam through the Greyhound lines from El Paso to
Sacramento to Gilroy to Cupertino to Escondido to Vista to
Stockton to Ramona all the way here. We take a smoky de-
light in the mountainous regions of bus stations, train stops
and late night restaurants.

Look around.

This is the town where I learned how to bowl at midnight.

I used to go with María Martínez every week. She's a Chicana girl with no mother and a father called Ambrosio who
waits on tables at Hotel Circle every night. Ambrosio wears
black wool robes and stands in the center of a *Penitente* flay-
ing mound in his dreams, he comes home at about two in the
morning, slips under the door spreading fever across María's
night, guarding her soft percale sheets. He kisses her on the
neck as he closes his eyes.

*I didn't weep when your mother died; I never thought she
would go so soon, María. We were going to name your
brother Fidencio, after the famous healer of Zacatecas, but
she stopped breathing and his little chest must have fallen
back into the deep seas searching for the shattered light of
the moon and now all I have is you and this reddish wool
robe that has grown over my shoulders. Every evening when I
come home it flowers another sheet around my heart. I will
never forgive her for leaving me. She knows I will never tell*

*you this. How can I, María? Where would I begin? You will
only know the weight of this woven father I carry over my
soul. Good night, my darling María.*

This is the apartment house where I live. Bobby and Billy
Pridemore like bowling, too. They are the only guys I know
with a Tennessee accent. Their dad, Woody, works at the Na-
val shipyard at the end of Broadway Street. I think Bobby,
the oldest, told me that they are from Nashville. Or was it
Knoxville?

Bowling pins.
The Greyhound exhaust and the unforgiving tearing leaves
    of every door.
María.
Sidewalk penitents. Waiters and washerwomen.
A blue vulture vouching for his brother, Mayor P. Wilson.
City Hall.
The black light popping behind your back.

These are the signboards and minstrels standing at
    the curb.
Listen. Even Milton, the muscular street cat breathes in
    this stirring
moonlight. You can see him behind Pearson's parking lot.
Call him out now:

*Turn the gold coins in your eyes
Open the secret onyx of the ocean inside you.
And blow. It is time.*

I work at the Saint James Retirement Hotel on the corner of
8th and F streets. I am a dishwasher boy at $1.25 an hour. I go
in twice a week and on weekends. I clean up the floors of the
cafeterias and with metal wool barbs I scrub the giant pots
and pans and the stove grill. It's a mess. I try to break the
monotony by switching on the AM. The hit song, *Don't Mess*

with Bill, spins as I cut my fingers on a tin bowl. A tall old
Swede showed me the ropes. No one says nothing. It's a four-
teen-story building. And at exact intervals of the day the ash-
colored beings are wheeled to the bottom-floor lobby to sit in
front of the blue tunnel where westerns and dragnets shoot
and jangle into puppets on their laps. Then, in another rect-
angle in the basement, an appointed person in a white shirt
pushes the old ones into the chow hall to shake their forks for
eggs and apricot marmalade. I am here after everyone leaves.
I'm the night boy. Go in at eight and come out at twelve. Half
of my body is wet. And I walk to this house. Ten blocks. The
cops usually stop me. They taunt me with their long nose,
chrome teeth:

Where are you going?
What's a schoolboy walking "F" Street at this hour?
Hey, come here, what's your name?

My record

is my business. I want to tell them bend down fellas, hear the
air spilling out of the antenna holes in your eyes. Do you
know what time it is? Time to open your hood, fellas: feed the
spotted-red salamander or it will leap out from the manifold.
It's getting so cold in there, and the gator-drop wants to be a
gator-sky someday, soon.

This has always been a city of blue coiled ambitions. A million babies lie awake across the fluttering mattresses in the
dim lobbies of the theaters, tossing and turning, staring at the
wet bulbs of brown light burning above them, praying for a
tall man with two warm handfuls of milk, but he will never
come.

I was named after my grandmother Juanita Martínez Palo-
márez. My great-grandmother's name is Viventa Palomares.

My mother carried their tresses in a pillow case for thirty-six years; then one day she burned them over her small stove.

This is where I live.

III. Visitations

You really want to know something? Take a look over there. See? The old man Ho, who always wears a pale avocado green cardigan taped to his shoulders; he has a secret. Listen: he has a child, Laura. A three-year-old daughter. Eyes, inscrutable as the inside wanderings of a sea anemone. I have seen her hands. She draws like a Renaissance master. Da Vinci hands. I tell you, I know. In seven years she will have a draft for a new technology of surfaces and glass-fiber laser lenses. She will invent the arc of peace between the Soviets and the North American machine. And—I know it—twenty years from now, she will come face to face with the Great Mad Retro-Virus, killer of skin and the world. And what will she do?

Mr. Ho knows.

Today I saw him go out to the back of his store. He sat down in his little chair and he looked out past the tin cans and the busted 7-Up bottles piled against the shed musing with the mosquitoes and the flies. He pulled out a Lucky Strike. And as he clipped the matchstick with his thumbnail for a spark, a streak of slow sunlight filtered over his girl, crawling out of the spearmint patch. He sat motionless; the matchstick fell for miles into the weeds. Listen. You must listen.

This is the Year of the Blowfish.

Blowfish goes into the bathroom with a snuck-in copy of *Gent,* or naked torsos that it snatches cut out from Jack's Bookstore on Broadway Street. Blowfish swims deep into this glossy theater room of sink-tub-toilet-mirror illuminations.

There, in the aquamarine, an octopus of saliva, sperm, and hot water slapping over its pebbled skin. Filaments, sheaths. Everything blurs into orange lipstick waves in the lungs, a car crash against reddish thighs; this basement shore dwellers know as America.

I live downtown

in the Empire of rare visitations; between the visionary plea- sure of the beggar and the buried passions, abandoned hands, wicker flesh.

IV. Topaz

My father is 82 years old. A quiet man that I secretly love. He will sit and read from the Baptist Bible sometimes, and my mom tells stories of a Catholic asylum—long ago. I live in a temple of proverbs.

Come tu pan con gozo y vivirás

Cain's eye

Juventud, divino tesoro

I want to tell my dad that I love him.

He is friendly. He's a tall and fair-skinned man whose cheeks flush easily. An orphan from a small village in Chihuahua. His hands are made out of shiny tree bark. You can see the different maps of colored wood. Every now and then when the *Reuma* gets him he puts on his copper bracelet. In the mornings, after he fries some potatoes and eggs, he goes out for a jaunt on one of those trains he used to take when he worked as a cowboy in Cheyenne, Wyoming, way down- town to talk with his friend, Mr. Kelly. *La Plazita*. It's right across the Cabrillo theater and Bradley's hamburgers. He's

always out there with his buddies. Sometimes, my mom goes
with him.

Me and my momma and daddy.
We could easily sing, hum, and tell stories all year long. They
know about my algebra, but it's my school stuff and I keep it
to myself. On Saturdays, in the summer, we'll take a big nap
on the floor. Anyone busting in would think we had just
taken a bottle of sleeping pills to end the deadly patter of
living on Welfare. My mother has these pains that doctors
can't figure out so she can't work. She's a lot younger than my
pop. But, she loves to be doing things all the time.

I look at her.

Topaz is her favorite color.
Her eyes sparkle and her voice is small as she is;
a rare voice, a leaf violin.

She laughs at my faces.

My Anthony Quinn face. My Emmet Kelly face. My Charlie
Chaplin face. And then I got this bag of family faces: Uncle
Ferni who collects wristwatches and transistor radios under
the bed; Uncle Chente who seethes darkly and asks cops
for the definition of Misery; Aunt Tere who goes swimming
every morning and drinks a lot of milk; my almost Aunt
Alvina who stomps through the kitchen, puts unbearable pep-
pers in the soup and when she's in the restroom she doesn't
care if she leaves the door open.

In the year of the Blowfish laughter is necessary.
Clean living is good.

V. Half

Half-brothers

and half sisters don't count. I got a bunch in New Mexico. I
hate them. They own my father's land and they own what
they call their home. Next year they are coming to my father's funeral. They are going to look at my mother with the
eyes of landlords. And they are not going to say a stinking
word to her or to me. They will choose a metallic blue casket,
some flowers, and a corsage at the 6th Street mortuary and
they will write a check for the undertaker and they will walk
away the next day to a rented car. And we will burn for
years.

Then I will call the *Plazita* Gypsies, the homeless of the City;
tell them to come with their honey-glazed guitars, to come
dressed with roses and emerald-green wreathes around their
hips. I will ask them to paint their dresses and Levis with yellow peacocks, tell them that I will carry the porcelain vases
of sweet milk and the large plates of glowing fish. My mother
and I will lay on an oak wood table beneath father's favorite
eucalyptus tree and trace the star-shaped darkness.

I have many faces.

Lorca & Chubby Checker
Pedro Infante & Shirley Maclaine
Jerry Lewis & Agustín Lara
Emile Griffith & Marilyn Monroe
El Santo & Roy Rogers
St. Judas & JFK
La Vírgen de Guadalupe & John Lennon
The Wolfman & Shirley Temple
Sartre & Godzilla
The King of Tijuana & the Queen of Vietnam
Picasso & Sidney Poitier

Wordsworth & Richie Valens
LeRoi Jones & Simone de Beauvoir
Caravaggio & Andy Warhol
Magritte & Martin Luther King
Schopenhauer & Doris Day
Janis Joplin & Lucille Ball
Desi Arnaz & Sam Cooke
Tina Turner & El Santo Niño de Atocha
Borges & James Brown.

The only face I leave untouched is Doña Osorio's.
Do you know Doña Osorio? She lives next door.

She's a good friend of my moms. She's about 91 years old.
Sturdy. Light hazel eyes, saddening. Her apartment is a mu-
seum of sorts. Thick-lipped green glass jars filled with wide-
milky-white buttons and tarnished silver bracelets. Candies
wrapped tightly over small plates colored in pastels. Perfume
bottles lined up against the mirror in front of her bed. A dark
wide-hipped guitar. She shows me. I've taken a couple of lessons from her. It was my mom's idea. There is a strange feeling in the room. Doña Osorio has measured every chamber,
every stairway of sound. I can smell something burning when
I visit her. I want to tell her something very dear to us is on
fire. I want to hold her small shoulders closely and whisper
to her.

Our world is burning Doña Osorio. All the strings of all the
guitars are snapping. Outside a funnel widens. A funnel into
earth. Into the sea. There's a terrible flame with its spiked
white knife beckoning all of us. Your perfumes are boiling
Doña Osorio.

(She turns and speaks)

Find the hidden room in this house, at dawn, and go there. The
dark guitar with a green ribbon at the neck will lean toward

*you. All my favorite flasks half-filled with black honey will
thicken. A spotted, blue cup will raise its candle eye. And you
will hear the rain drape this ground, this cave, the country.*

I love Richie Valens.
So does my mom. Sometimes, when I am playing *La Bamba*
on my guitar she starts to dance, swiveling her wrists in
the air, her eyes looking up and her mouth biting a rose.

Half of my body is barracuda. Honest.

The other half

is violet orchid. I swim and crackle. I keep still and glide
across this kingdom of fishnet hearts, lamps made out of
Jewish-Mexican chest skin and helmeted yellow fire hydrants
standing at guard by electric confetti bars. 2nd and Broadway.
I take out my camera.

Do the swim, baby!

It's a groove. You have to leave the pad at 9 a.m. on Saturday.
You walk all the way down "C" Street to *La Plazita*. There,
you take the R bus, sit in the back and read a few passages
out of *Nausea*. Love the cover, right? When you get there it's
about 58 degrees. You check out the scene. A few surfers. A
couple of dogs are chasing the thin-legged birds. Seagulls curl
their heads beneath their wings thinking about algebra,
homework, maybe. You kick back and you lay down on your
watermelon-striped towel and you turn on your twelve-
transistor box radio. You got a plan. First,

I'll lay around looking like I am reading. Then, I'll listen to
KCBQ crooning songs like *Kansas City* and *These Boots Are
Made for Walking*. I'll rub some Coppertone on my bod. I
love the smell. It's like I just stepped out of a coconut malt.
Mmmmmm.

I bet you the dogs can't figure me out. They probably think I am a funny banana with legs or something. I'll wait 'till it gets super hot! I'll start to sizzle. Two hours is max, ok? Then, I'll do my famous Tab Hunter surfer sprint to the waves man! I'll dive in like they do in the *Wonderful World of Sports* on channel 2, with my arms arched into a bird beak cutting the waves. Yeah! And then, I'll come up on the other side of the cool wall and I'll be acting like I am waiting for the big one, the monster one. I'll be the suave guy in the middle of the ocean. It'll be around 1:30 by now. My fingers will puff bloated bread sticks. I'll have a tuff suntan. All the bitchin' girls will be on their toes with their hands over their foreheads as if saluting an admiral coming home from war. They'll be screaming about the handsome guy catching the tallest curl in the history of Silver Stand Bay. I'll be debonair like

in the *Salem* cigarette commercials. I'll come in with lumbering tawny shoulders, a rusty beard and a sailor's honest smile like Anthony Quinn or Burt Lancaster, and I'll mumble something to the girls like *La Dolce Vita Bambina*. And with the ease of a buck-toothed Louis Jordan, I'll lay down on one elbow, singing a couple of songs in Italian, and I'll open up a bamboo basket and pull out a soft salami-and-tomato submarine sandwich and a Pepsi.

I am looking up at the sky.

I can't believe I am graduating next year. I can't believe it. My hair squeaks as I comb it with my fingers. Breathe in hodad, that's right, expand that chest. Saturdays are your lucky days. Breathe out. The shore a Dufy watercolor mirror. *Blow.*

VI. Linda Light

I ditched school.

I went over to Linda Light's house on University Street and did it for the first time. She's German. I am a Chicano. She's a senior. I am a junior. We've been going out on and off for the last couple of months. Haven't told anyone, not even Memo Urista, my best buddy who's still wondering how to do it.

I hid in Linda's attic all night. It was terrible. Crouched, hugging my knees in a cave of boxes full of cold cans. Creamed corn? Vegetarian beans? Army rations in case a bomb rumbles into the military base a few miles north? Cans in the attic and me. Maybe this was the necessary stage for the beginnings of a novel like Mr. Wightman, my English Lit teacher, had suggested.

Excerpt from the *Blowfish* Novel:

*The dark cans & me, a brown boy in a
cubicle replicating itself into minute
cylindrical tunnels; meticulous wombs,
tribal tubers, restraining an inner
cyclone of red honey and spore jelly.
Infinite casings with sparkling lips,
fuzzy tendrils curling out from a belly-
buttonless new god; a green-eyed brain
smoldering, each convolution of the lobe
emitting faint spirals of vapor that will
not live unless I crack and push through
the intricate metal fiber sheathe that
separates us from Nirvana.*

Hours later.
I pissed on myself. Too much Coca-Cola on a Friday night. Damn it! It's the worse thing in the world! When Linda finally opened the attic floor door (now that her parents had gone to work at about seven in the morning) I stunk like a wino. I couldn't stand up. My back had molded into charred mahogany. And my pants suddenly unraveled two spotted-green cellophane cocoon legs. Dazed.

The blond peach fuzz on her breasts is still on my mind?
What was it doing there? That is the crux of the matter.
Memo will never figure it out. He's been collecting nasty car-
toons all along so he can have a ready-made set of fun posi-
tions in case one doesn't fire right. What shall I tell him?
Asshole.

Linda, her staunch German parents, who don't like brown
boys, her luminous attic, and me are going to split next year.
It'll happen outside the zoo parking lot. She'll be coming out
of work, strutting towards her black '56 Plymouth. I'll be
waiting for her and for some crazy reason I'll say something
like "this is it." And she'll let it ride for a second. This is it?
She'll look at me with her brilliant blues, for a second.
The camera focus will go into wide angle:

Linda Light drives north with a windshield spattered with fast
patterns; the old eucalyptus trees on Roosevelt street remembers. Fluttering shadows. Golden spears flash, then spill into
the air.

I walk south,

back to my apartment, passing the old museums by the zoo
with their carved Franciscan priests and porous clay angels
without the iris in their eyes. I go back, over the bright slopes
of Pepper Grove at the edge of the playground. Remember
when Benny Vanilla duked it out with Danny Flores? Everybody cut school early. The casual stand-bys thought we were
the new science fair kids on the way to the Aerospace building! Now, nothing moves here except the muscular wind and
the faint timbre of things, rustling, invisible animals tracking
through the underbrush and these odd footsteps still digging
fantasy and rage into the gravel.

I stop at the old open theater, next to the slide and the
swings. It is very dark, even in the early afternoon. I go in

further. I look back to the empty merry-go-round. There is a back room with a velvety black tunnel. Twisted and burnt weeds in odd clumps on the floor. Linda

thanks for inviting me out to dance. (Earlier in the evening we had beef stroganoff at Mr. A's on Fifth. What a date! It was worse than making a replica of the USS Kittyhawk with q-tips! Stroganoff! Sounds like snake innards in vinegar.) I never expected anyone to ask me out. You even had the nerve to ask me in Spanish class. Shit! I was hoping Mercy Gómez would ask me. She was in the third row though. Tell your mom who's name I don't know and your dad who's name I don't know that everything is alright. I will dance alone; here in this crazy wooden room of wild stems and blown-out walls. Tell them your love is a memory, a fresh hive clasped by two naked hands and then tossed back and forth through the gray arcs of time.

I cross the bridge dividing North Park and Downtown. The freeway thickens and I walk further into my place. The ocean at Silver Strand Bay is silent now. I scribble a lot of things here. Most of the time, though, I am looking at what's about to blow.

VII. Neo-Fauvism

(I paint in bold colors. Someday I will start a Neo-Fauvist theater.)

Mrs. Steiger in my art studio class knows this. She says that even if it costs her her job she will stand up for my kind of stuff. I am not kidding. Last semester I did a large 6' x 4' cross painted with white enamel, and nailed a Brown-black rubber doll baby at its heart dripping red-dyed varnish from the left side of its thin chest. There was so much luster in that artificial wound. Even the school faculty came to quiz me to make sure the baby wasn't dangerous. They were wondering what kind of shirt was necessary to dress him up. I told them I

bought the doll at the "D" Street thrift shop. Dolls are real.
Señora Osorio knows. I told them that they had missed the
point. Brown-black doll has words. Brown-black doll speaks

(Two years from now):

*Mexican President Díaz-Ordaz gives military orders. Crush
the students, burst the soft spot in their forehead. Shatter
thousands into blue flesh; let their families swim with the
tattered lights; their last wide-eye searching for kin. May no
one ever again hear this Aztec anthem.*

*There will be a mural on every street of Mexico splayed
against asphalt. Look: red-orange arms, a sudden burst from
the silver-sequined knit shawls, poster paint screeching
through shrapnel, fingernails, the cartoon monster, Kalimán,
stalking Plaza Tlatelolco screaming with the voice of Lorca*

My Brown-black doll looks into the air. Patterdale—bends in
the fire. The best portion of a good boy's life, his little, nameless, unremembered acts. O little dark doll, look there, into
the storm cloud over the sea:

Zapata's nightmare

and the fat politico's dream for American membership into
the beautiful wet bar of rape, champagne, *haciendas* sewn in
spandex and dacron. Style like Elvis.

O little dollbaby,
this is the umber mist that hangs above our century. Listen
again—

someone spins the gramophone: come here, my love let's
dance to the Blood Waltz of the Landless, this watery frenzy
among the multitudes—pelvic mutilations—spirit and sex
denied to the Earth Virgin.

Sweet lacquered child,
let us roam across the shredded roadways and small-town
food markets flooding with the uncombed heads of lettuce
and desire. Who will drive a '58 Dodge Coke distributor truck
to quench the innumerable stations in our wastelands?

How long shall we remain window shoppers for a nation? I
want a falcon to lift us above these chasms, these flaming
woods, the pop of carriages and gears. Now,

look there, hiding behind your doll dress, someone says,
Sweetheart, please.

he says, *we don't want to be late to the soccer game of
humble beggars and one-eyed Mexican poets selling chewing
gum for more North American tanks and grenades.*

Do we have time darling? Someone else says:
Will we make it? Hurry, call a taxi! Later,

*we'll go to the regatta, you probably prefer this. And we'll sit
as all regatta lovers sit. On an olive-green bench looking over
a quiet pond, hedgerow, little lines of sportive wood running
wild; a tuft in the middle, a camouflaged abyss and there you
will toss a pear, a wish for the sacred goldfish. Raoul Dufy
will come to mind. Your arms will bristle in this sandstone
light. Dufy painted regattas. He also painted orchestras and
seasidescapes.*

You-someone: Which do you think is the most beautiful?
Blowfish: *Vaullaris*, of course.
You-someone: I didn't know you knew about things like that?
Blowfish: I learned about it in Mr. Petrich's art class . . . a
long time ago.
You-someone: You still remember that stuff?
Blowfish: It was the only class worth walking into and maybe
Mr. Wightman's.

You-someone: Is he the guy you said read *Peanuts* with dark
glasses on every morning?
Blowfish: If I ever become a teacher I am going to do the
same thing!
You-someone: What is *Vaullaris* anyway, Peanutman?
Blowfish: I don't know . . .
A formalist critic writes:

> "Two notable series of seasidescapes date from the 1920s. Some of
> the paintings are dark umber, having to do with the icy light of
> the North; some are night scenes reminiscent in their blackness
> of the ominous core of a savage masterpiece like the deserted
> garden of a decade before; others are in a much more southern
> vein of a blue and radiant economy. None of these is more poetic
> than the evocative *Vaullaris* in which an arcade merges with the
> sky in a perfect metaphor of open-to-the-air-summer-life. B.F./
> pp. 58."

(In twenty years, some guy with the collar up
is going to write this in one of those toilet paper Bible fantasy
magazines).

You-someone: And he's going to miss the whole point isn't he?
Blowfish: Look closely.

Abandonment.

Absence.

Brown-black doll speak to me:
Is it a talcum-colored building between reef and sky carried
in the air by the sunset and blood serum pillars? Is this our
night realm, our purer world? (Look at the damn thing
closely!) Is it an enemy fortress pillaged by the jungle? Or better yet, by the vengeance of the last tribes still living on
maize, salt, plantain, and oblong green gourds of apple fla-
vors? The Last Indians of the Peripheries? Look there, you can

see the parachutes falling from the skies into the Highland tropical forests.

Another army searches out the exiles from the captive villages. Scorched; the calves, razor cut, flayed patches, loosened milk; tree bark in the bone.

The Village Council has been executed. Even the village translators, *Los Promotores*, The Karibu Bush are hanging from the vines.

No one walks in the cityscape to the left.
The villagers have eaten their fingers. Place names—*Morazán, Quito, Johannesburg* are scrawled on every lounge mirror. Lipstick mixed with hair gel. The village children are watering the sidewalks and there in the fissures of cement, the seedlings suckle; a fetus glows and revels in glory, O Brown-black doll, give her milk.

Go in now.

VIII. Photography

Sometimes after dinner there's nothing better than stretching out a bit. Take out your camera, let the eye relax, form its own prism, envelope its own sweet diffractions; a rouge frame worn down, erased by the years, smoke, the wingspan of its own glass dream.

Sometimes
after dinner, there's nothing better than stretching out a bit and going out with mom and dad, walk as all villagers walk and witness the shooting lights of the forest, listen to its grief and receive a trace of its ceremonial embrace. My father walks ahead. And there, upon the makeshift platform, the depot. In the center

stands the wooden image of *Salem*, cigarette queen, and her consort, the Redcap Boy who rules the luggage of all visitors from the Peripheries. Both are dressed in purple and gold trappings. The back corridors of the depot are made to open to a series of intricate canals and bridges. The entire building is gaudily decorated with football posters, dinner plates, mirrors, and numbers.

We sit and pretend
to be going somewhere. We even get up and go over to the small chrome diner, order apple pie a-la-mode and coffee. I hang out, buy some *Walnettos* and shoot pictures of myself at the photo-booth. I used to bring María Martínez here, especially on New Year's. That's when this place really swings. All the sailors are out getting dragon tattoos. Even my Uncle Ferni comes out here and buys watches after the holidays. He says you got to time it right. He even raids the lockers in the depot and usually comes home with a duffel bag that some weary Navyman forgot on leave. Mr. Petrich, my art teacher, would like it here, too.

There's an amber light that touches everything; a faraway fire that kindles the skin and filters a bronze fairness into the eyes; the old one's faces become larger, kinder almost; all the bodies seem to twist rather than tilt across expansive planes. Hesitations, wishing tongues, half-spoken joys criss-cross in every shirt button.

Cimabue would find his taciturn Madonna bitten by the years and El Greco, his spiraling crucifixions, here, in this palace of destinations, there—by Mrs. Paz Márquez, the hotel maid, over there by Mrs. Pickett who broke her teeth while skating as a girl. There is even a fortuneteller inside a glass box six feet high. I call her *Siwanava* after the Goddess of Streams and Lost Children;

give her a silver token and you will see.
Give her a small lance from your hotel refrigerator, meat
dishes, boiled rice from the Moon Cafe on Fourth Street and
she will give you a parchment map.

*Siwanava, Siwanava, here's a Walnetto, all I have for you to-
day, tell me if you can, lift up your delicate ivory hand and
with your opal ring point to the great star where María's lost
brother lives, remember him this night, gaze into your rivers,
into your palm fronds, into the long, blue, quiet beak of the
lake fog, be merciful, do not hesitate, place your mouth
against this glass, no one is looking, tell me and I will press
my ear and listen. Everyone is asleep on the benches, they are
in their canoes headed for your waters, is little Fidencio
there, is he there above the jukebox, listening to Elvis's "One
Night" spinning among the grass reeds?*

Only tremors. Tremors again. I can feel them in my arms. In
this sea.

I am always at the magazine counter looking at the new cars
of the year, *True Confessions*, movie stars and the wigs the
cashier wears. We leave around 9 p.m. But, it's open all night
and it's free.

Mr. Dwayne Ho never lets his kids out here. He doesn't want
them to catch a cold. I think he knows about the Retro-Virus,
maybe *Siwanava* told him. I wish I had another Walnetto. I
like how they stick to your teeth.

I can hear little Laura speaking a forest language, I think she
imitates birds when they are in danger:

*No one knows how to cure the Retro because it goes into you,
there, inside your arms when they open and then it bites into
your cells, a funny miniature television changing the chan-
nels of your cell's eye so it can't be shut off. And there it*

grows, multiplies until your body is another picture, your
lungs fill with gray liquid and the limbs and skin burn; pic-
ture a knotted bedsheet, a crushed refrigerator cardboard box
shot with open sores. Twenty years from now Retro will wash
up on the shore. Transparent, filmy, in a plastic syringe or in
a government laboratory vial, raw unfiltered, uncooked, out-
side of flesh or blood and there inside the fine sheathes of
steel it will boil underneath the microscope, it will wait to be
assigned and given orders to infiltrate the round lips of sons
and daughters, to bury a village; this is the unknown soldier
and it will sever them from their mother and their father and
from each other and slowly the earth shall lift its sad breast
and weep. The summer will be over soon.

What will I do?

I just may join up with my uncle Chente. Last year he invited
me to travel with him in his beat-up red panel truck. He says
he'll teach me sculpture and silk-screen. Drop school? I don't
know, he always has paint on his nose. And the beach? But,
who wants to work at the St. James? Or maybe, I'll just stay
here, work hard at my drawing. Shoot a portrait of Janis
Joplin?

IX. Checklist

Ambrosio's hungers
Imaginary brothers and sisters
Funny Banana
Graduation
Tribal tubers
The baroque eye of the Franciscan priest
Brown-black doll lying awake above our century
Regatta blue-green
Gel on every wall
Siwanava—offerings

Sun crystals for Mr. Duane Ho
Walnettos
Finish my paper for Mrs. Conant's Bio class

X. Habitat

Mrs. Conant, Biology.

BLOWFISH (draft)

THE BLOWFISH IS ONE OF THE MOST MYSTERIOUS, DEADLY, ~~BEAUTIF~~ FISH IN THE SEA. IT IS AN EVIL, SPOTTED, SPECKLED MONSTER, ATTACKING AND DESTROYING THE SOFTER, THIN SHELLED CREATURES IN ITS MIDST.

NO ONE KNOWS THIS. ~~THE GULLIBILITY OF TH~~ HE SURVIVES ON THE GULLIBILITY OF OTHERS. ~~THEY SEE~~ THEY DO NOT NOTICE HIS STONY BEAK; HOW IT GRINDS IN THE DEPTHS, THEY NEVER HAVE SEEN HIS BUCK TOOTH RAZORS, HIS POWERFUL CHEWING MUSCULATURE. THE ~~THE~~ SUNDRY INHABITANTS OF HIS ENVIRON ~~ARGUE~~ PREFER TO ARGUE, EVEN PHILOSOPHIZE ON THE COLOR OF HIS ODD EYES. SOME SAY IRIDESCENT, BLUE-GREEN. OTHERS ARE RESOLUTE; BROWN, PLAIN BROWN, THEY PUFF AT THE COLLAR. THE WISE ONES ADD THAT ~~ONLY IN LIGHTER DENSITY THAT HE~~ THE BLOWFISH EYE DARKENS IN LIGHTER SHORE LIGHT. THERE ARE A FEW THAT NEVER SPEAK OF THE BLOWFISH: THE CLOISTERED, SOFT-BELLIED, MOLLUSKS. ~~THEY MEREL~~ IT IS SAID THAT THEIR MUTE, OBLONG FIGURE IS THE RESULT OF HAVING SEEN THE SPINY TENTACLE NOSE THAT PROPS THE BLOWFISH SPECTRAL EYES. YET, THE MAJORITY OF THESE WAYFARERS OF THE SEA RIDICULE THE ~~BLO BL SPECKLED~~ GLOBEFISH. HE LACKS TABLE MANNERS, HE EATS WIRE, PLASTIC CORD, HOOKS OF ALL SIZES—EVEN POISONOUS WORMS. HE GOES AS FAR AS LETTING BULLY FISH SWALLOW HIM.

~~THEY DON'T KNOW.~~
THEY DON'T KNOW HE IS A PATIENT BOY; A WELL-GROOMED BOY WITH DARK THINGS INSIDE OF HIM; THAT HIS EYES CAN SEE ~~INTO~~ THROUGH THE COSMIC SHEATHS THAT ENVELOPE HIM. IT DID NOT OCCUR TO THE OTHERS THAT THE OCEAN IS THE PLIABLE PHOSPHOR BOARD WHERE HE PLAYS HIS MASTER GAME. THERE, ON THAT WEBBED SLATE HE PRACTICES, HE

REHEARSES THE ACTUAL DESTRUCTION OF THE WORLD AND THE EMERGENCE OF A NEW UNIVERSE.

HE LETS THE ENEMY SWALLOW HIM. THEN ONCE INSIDE THE QUIVERING ~~COLD~~ FLESH, HE BEGINS TO EXPAND BY SIPPING THE JUICES UNTIL HE IS THREE TIMES HIS ORIGINAL SIZE. THE ENEMY FISH STRETCHES, TEARS, AND BLOWS INTO ~~NOTHINGNESS~~ NOTHING. BLOWFISH ESCAPES ONCE AGAIN INTO HIS OWN WATERS, ULTRAMARINE. IN THIS WAY HE GAINS KNOWLEDGE, LEARNS THE COSMIC LESSONS WELL.

VICTORIANO MARTÍNEZ

SHOES

Out of all our enemies, all the catastrophes of nations
scattered to rubble, plowed over with salt, we still have
the warm friendliness, the unrelenting spirit
of our shoes to console us.

Two bubbles, chopped square out of shapeless emptiness,
how this invention hisses in a hurry to correct time,
pumping little sneezes of sympathy for our tardiness.

Although they owe us nothing, they walk
in many of our dreams, conjuring music
from a vaporous sidewalk, or standing
as pure reverence
over the peaceful herds of our dead.

They, who always return back to us, faithfully,
from every tropic, every desert,
take up their jobs as stealth for the burglar,
spring under the killer's crouch, courage
for the guerrilla. They guard us
against thistles and thorns, protect us from stone
and the unseen disasters of glass.

Wheels mean nothing to the shoe. They are the first
of peasants and would never think to kneel
before any god, or suck up to whatever tablet of the Law.
Ravenous for distance, they supply whole lives
with the loss of a mere heel,
yet wear death, only once.

ALONG THE RIVER

There are sunrises where everything that pains us, leaves.
Where one's arm twisted on a question,
unravels its answer, and the fraction of a face becomes
    whole.

The sun blossoms shards of glass opposites everywhere,
yet none of them touches us.
We are in a forest, gummed together by light,
beside a river whose currents are feathers
twittering to become wind
before the sun shreds them madly to their source.

And after the seedless sowing of late afternoon shadows,
when the forest moves at the speed the sun pulls,
we say, This
is what I am: a sky of frightened birds,
an unmapped constellation of pores,
morning and night
forever stroking the wheel with each hand—
sun, moon, all the rest.

THERE'S NO STOPPING

The future that flares from a pistil is the seed
scorching to earth. While darkness leans
against the wind, and trees arrive
on the lip of distance the sun spreads on the road
for travelers, the seed makes itself known.

It demands water, and so reservoirs open
in a cloud. It discovers navigation in the stars,
begins the spurious journey through an intestine

or on a wing, between the brotherhood of dust
and heaven on a hill of dung.

Sure the moon gives its zero percent,
the sun its measure and water its spoon,
but the seed is at war with History
that wants to consume it, with Astronomy
that seeks to count its graves.

What does it matter that a man cradles under
a tree and celebrates with worms? Who cares
that ink fails? The seed must keep on
with its endless quarrel between ovule and sperm,
peeling up the crusts of asphalt and popping
like corn on the sidewalk, because the tumors
of the city must be destroyed, above all,
they must be annihilated—

so when trees chatter and conspire with rain,
and sweep like rivers down from the hills
the seed knows, it knows, there's no stopping.

RAIN

When clouds send rain to count everything they own,
every pore opens, every window breathes with the blur
of animals, thinking.
Cars hiss along the blooded teeth of neon.
So click the radio dead, dot the television black, and listen
instead, to the soft sucking of soil
under a dialect of leaves, listen
as clouds scribble notes for the music of sky.

There's no sadness, no fingers weeping through the leaves.
There's only a mouth through which the wind
sings; it is a hat tumbling down the street.

Rain, clattering on the slat-board fences,
curving under eyebrows and smacking foreheads
with the warm milk of memory's tit.
Down your chest, down your legs it
pours the salt of history
to chill along the sidewalk and waterfall
in a gutter.

      And then it swells, and waters move.
Business kneels to its mud and houses built on trust
wash down the slopes on the tips of its wing—
even you, there, listening
to the excited tongues of the elm tree, know
that every last breath of dust you own
will return to the forests from where it came.

ALPHABET

Out in the blue syringe of afternoon, among the cataract
clouds and blustering eucalyptus, the day
isn't all bliss and morning-glories; it isn't all
nuded trees rising in a praise to form. No, the day
is a page written up: cars in conjunction and
people-periods behind a desk
or as scraps of adjective swarming the sidewalks.

The year is a book which can never be read
the same way twice.
You open its pages and thirst crowds
in the breathless soil of Africa. You close its pages,

and there you are, a tiny decimal
surrounded by zeros
that will never multiply nor bruise the world.

You open its pages again, and locusts pop
like seed, to rain down desert
over the last green jewels. You close its pages
and there you are, again, standing
by a window,
just as you've stood by a window for these many
years, looking out and waiting;
a statue looming forever out to sea, you wait
for this age to ignite ink in your spine,
so you can curl into alphabet, and be done with it.

BARBARA RENAUD GONZÁLEZ

THE SUMMER OF VIETNAM

So, what are you writing about? I ask Bill Broyles, the former *Newsweek Magazine* goldenboy. He's the Texas man who can write *anything* and get it published. Unlike me.

"Vietnam," he says. The worst answer. The only answer that can make me cry.

Instead, at night I remember.

Ernesto Sánchez is Vietnam to me. Born July 9, 1947. In a place called Kennedy, Texas. Died in the summer of 1967, somewhere in Vietnam. Somewhere in my 13th summer.

This is my Vietnam.

I sang love songs to them. Made up Ken dolls after them. Imagined kissing them. I still do. Marine-boys. Boys in dress green with stiff brass buttons that would catch your breaking heart when they gave you the biggest *abrazo* of your life. Then they died in Vietnam.

Always teasing me. "This last dance is for you, Barbara," they'd say. Taught me to dance those skip-steps of adolescence. Told me they'd wait for me. And they never came back from Vietnam to see how I'd grown up for them.

I knew they would not die. Heroes don't die in the movies, after all. The good guys always win. Who would dare extinguish the crooked smiles, football hands and Aqua Velva faces I knew so well? My brothers-at-war.

Of the 3,427 Texas men who died in Vietnam, 22 percent were Latinos. And another 12 percent of the dead were African-American. The minorities were *not* a minority in the platoons, but a majority of the frightened faces. And one-third of the body bags.

This at a time when Latinos constituted 12 percent of the population.

But the machismo goes a long way in war. We Latinos received more medals, thirteen of the prestigious Medal of Honor, than any other group.

We can count soldiers in the American Revolution (as Spaniards), the Roosevelt Rough Riders, both sides of the Civil War, and plenty of fathers and abuelitos in the world wars. Soldiering doesn't require U.S. citizenship, and no one cares how you crossed the border if you're willing to fight on our side.

We lost our best men in Vietnam. Isaac Camacho died first in 1963. Everett Alvarez was the first American pilot shot down, spending eight-and-a-half years as a POW. Juan Valdez was in the last helicopter leaving Vietnam. First in, and last out. They didn't go to Canada or Mexico. They went directly to Vietnam.

But from Oliver Stone, you would think that all our boys looked like Tom Cruise. Or agonized at China Beach. No. They were my brothers, uncles, cousins, my heroes.

Sometimes it looks as if they died for nothing. Impossible. It cannot be. Blood lost is blood redeemed, they say. What is the boy worth? If he died for all of us, then we must gain in proportion to the sacrifice. A Medal of Honor for the neighborhood school. Some Distinguished Service Crosses for family housing. Maybe the Bronze Stars for the judge or councilman. Flying Crosses for a good job. And a Purple Heart for a mother who still cries in Spanish.

MARIE-ELISE WHEATWIND

Los Perdidos

"Catalina"

Was that Catalina? It had been ten years, but I'd know those dark eyes in a wink: shining under the long strands of a black perm, nose crinkled slightly in a half-squint smile. Poised on the spiral stair at the Hyatt Regency Bar, coy and leggy and naturally tan, she waited till all eyes were on her, head tilted just right for admiration. I was caught in her spell. Was she suddenly shy? The bartender, handing me two beers, pointed one eyebrow in her direction, smirking "Check out the new Pro, sizing up the room . . . " then she nonchalantly turned and cruised through—slow and smooth, casting a caressing glance on every man.

How Catalina and I had practiced that casual attitude, our fourteenth summer at the city pool! "Watch me go swank down the gangplank," she'd whisper sideways from her open hand. "I'll give these pirates something to regret. . . . " Then she'd pretend to model the narrow length of the diving board, eyes dazed, seemingly oblivious, barely bouncing in her first two-piece, the green water alive with muscled flesh. By summer's end she'd outgrown the local pool, waving at me from a passing convertible on her way to the beach. Catalina had learned from her older sisters and cousins how to dress, what to say, when to seem helpless. Over the phone she'd whisper the nuances of teenage teasing, the mysteries of the French kiss.

Turning back to my work, I try to keep her in view in the bar mirror, all the while squeezing limes into four gin and tonics, arranging a handful of white napkins into overlapping petals on my tray, and planning a route that will cross her path long enough to grin "Hey Girl!" like we'd seen each other last week. But before I can set the drinks down and make change, three wine coolers have waved at me for another round, and a wedding rehearsal floats in, announcing "Champagne!" filling up the tables with pastel importance, while Catalina ascends the spiral stair on the arm of a handsome, well-tailored suit, laughing up at his face, never looking back.

DARREN J. DE LEÓN

EXTRA INNINGS

In front of everybody
Lil' Eddie liked to lick his ruca China's face.
He slid his dust-coated tongue
And puckered his drunk lips
To her pancaked olive skin.
He forced her to throb pistos
With the crew or to drive to the store
For more smokes when we were fucked up.
Her spider lashes weaved
Waves of young lust to us,
As we drank Old Gold
And chain-smoked Camels.

Chuey had small shoulders,
Almost as narrow as his neck;
Good for slipping through bars,
Broken windshields and warped garage doors.
He was the master of the Sunday night beer run.
When video kids would pack Asteroids with quarters,
And the Stop-n-Go clerk hawked the kids
Who ripped out naked scrapes of *Playboy*
We would park our hoop, "Flash '76," around the corner.
Toking-a-smoke, we'd jam when Chuey came running full
Bore. Smiling and panting as he jumped into the
Truck bed full of empties with two twelvers
Carried like Easter baskets.

Lil' Eddie's bottom lip dripped as he talked.
He wanted to go back alone to bang in Bloomas.
His blood was full of wack, his rag read
Like the brick flag facing our corner
"BH Y-Que."
His eyes held fourteen summers and
Had become only scars with raisins hid
Inside the slits. He listened to his old man,
Who had no thumbnails and had razored and inked
L-O-V-E H-A-T-E into his knuckles.
He talked about the vato he shot in a Fontana bar after work
How he learned to throw shoes in the state penta
And about being "In the Hole" with Sharky from Chino.
His scar-covered thumbs rubbed the chamber
As he handed me a filterless frajo.

I peddled home that night
With a stolen gun in my glove,
My cap flipped backwards.
My cleats hanging down from my neck.
I dreamed of naked olive skin and legs,
Of speeding life on a red-haired buzz,
Of scars on my face, of the day of my first shave
And never knowing that to throw bullets
Meant you'd have to catch them too.

LAWLESS PROSE

There are no laws in poetry
Only the word, a prisoner
Guilty of a barrage of verbs
Sprayed upon the target with ink.
The word this week is "Attica."

There are no laws in poetry
Only pen packers, flying off
Rounds of phrases that pierce
The skull, burrow the brain,
Exiting the mouth and fists.

There are no laws in poetry
Only the gangsters of page,
Carrying speared adjectives and
Sharply bladed nouns, chucking
Knowledge, killing innocence.

There are no laws in poetry
Only the fully loaded cannon
Of literature triggering the revolution,
Destroying the history of lies,
Restoring the balance to life.

There are no laws in poetry
Only volumes of aggression
Needed for oppression. Holy text!
Apart Hate does not read well.
The funniest things happen
                when I pull the trigger.

RAÚL NIÑO

FEBRUARY ON EIGHTEENTH STREET
For Judy Kirby

You told me about your father
his wonderful way of telling a story
you weren't too bad yourself
your whispers and your eyes

Do you remember
when the breeze
surprised us
with color and winter warmth?

That afternoon's generosity
giving us gold prisms from the sun
we paid in kind
with silver from our breaths

From east to west
on eighteenth street
no one measured
our steps

Daylight was short
after all it was February
still we made our way
slowly

While silhouettes of buildings
crossed the street
you said "look!"
we stopped as you pointed

II
San José del Cabo
on the tip of your tongue
growing before us
populating between each sentence

We stared at ourselves
two darkening reflections
in a pane of glass
behind it a map of Mexico

I watched your face
your lips began a story
your voice took my hand
a reflection grew in your eyes

There we materialized
Baja desert behind us
an ocean at our toes
the odor of waves filled us

I realized then
our lives have a smell
our past a lingering taste
like a guest moved in for good

Then you said
that things there had changed
"San José was not the same"
still you hoped to visit soon

III
Our walk in that amber hour
led us west where we found a church
framed between the cavity of two buildings
a massive Polish gray pointing skyward

Auspicious hands figured its belfry
over an immigrant community
when the Slavic language
was as far away from home

We saw its fading frescos
its wooden doors locked to evening
Saturday's approaching dusk
a separate solitude invading

Our distant gaze would not penetrate
those forest gates of religion
sealed from our innocence
as it was to our abandoned history

Yet you and I were still alive!
palms together our fingers embroidered
two strangers in unison
one body in prayer

Was it the texture of light
or lack of any familiar sounds
that seized us into becoming
pawns in a mean chronology?

    IV

Beneath memories of spring
the day retreated
into a slumbering earth
only then did I notice the ice

Cold chandeliers pointing down
a delicate suspension
clear stalactites from every light post
roof edges held their solid frailty

Christmas and New Years still
lingering in shop windows
scanty unwinding
those familiar dramas ending

Ours was a "promenade"
that was your word
what we began that afternoon
went against the current of dying

Near us obstinate shadows battled
I could feel them gaining
still we walked
our communion was living!

A threshold was just entering us
it was all a beginning then
we were warm within the chill
changing inside that season of ice

ORLANDO RAMÍREZ

THE AWAKENING

I.

I did not think them to be
my kind and loving family.
They were cartoons, the
characters who swallowed
dynamite and after the blast
were scorched and sarcastic.

Not my family, no, for I
was just a child (what did
my spine know of evil?) and
if I had known then I'd
spend the rest of my life
making excuses, I would have

traveled back, avoided the
zygote, detached myself from
the placenta. It would have
been goodbye, adios, auf
Wiedersehen. But knowledge
is not inherited. Stupidity

is and they tell me I am
the hope for a brave future.
I tell them I am no magazine
illustration, not one of
those kids like they see on
TV. No, my assault on the

world is this rope I lasso
about the legs of the
fleeing calf. I am the
fruition of the true dreams
of the mid-20th century.

2.

I met him one night driving
through the humid Valley of
Texas. His arm was out the
window, one hand on the
wheel, a song on his lips,
sex on his mind. I know you

don't trust me. No matter,
I know what I witnessed and
I know you agree, we never
know how the almighty will
represent their divinity.
Wisdom says I should have
killed him then and there
and, no doubt, if I had,
I would be a hero in some
parts of this world. But
I am a coward and he meant
no harm.

3.

I thought myself rootless,
no tendrils, no nutrition,
each police siren a song
to the arid night-time world
of grease and felt-made men,
products like the products

they buy. Oh, it was a
glorious machination to be
sitting as judge from a
window across the street from
a bar where telephone workers
met, then performed sex in

the alley. It was better than
TV, better than being a bird
or a bat, better than pictures
from Rio or North America. That's
when I realized I should have
murdered when I had the chance.

4.

I tell my son, "It is your
responsibility never to forgive
or forget." He thinks I am
describing the plot of another
old movie, something in black
and white. Whether you have

children or not, each day we
sacrifice. Today I have made a
nylon net of my heart and I
listen for the song of the
Hmong women crushing cans in
the alley and wait for the

repercussion to rise straight
into the fog like scissors to
slice a path to the afternoon
sun and I will wave my arms out
the window and the streetcars
will stop and the constellations

will dance for my little boy.

FOR YOUR FELLOW MAN

I don't want to hear about your drug problem.
Nobody listens to mine except the faucet, the
match and the remote control. Don't tell me

about your marriages because I haven't one to
tell. It's just me and the walls and the
pictures on the wall and the noise in between.

Please, I'm tired of you explaining away what
you did. I know about situations and tight
places and wanting to do the right thing.

I've tried myself and I end up chomping at
debts a mouthful at a time. I would love to
rob, to pillage, to scorn my betters or others.

But please, no more of your nonsense. I have
problems of my own and they have wings and they
sing from morning to night the same itchy

refrain and your noise just makes me crave
silence. No, more than that, intelligence, but
all I get is this chirping, this downloading

of information I neither want or need and that
grows rancid with each ticking day. So won't
you be quiet. For once. For your fellow man.

ENOUGH THAT

Who am I to complain?
Isn't it enough that
I keep my apartment
clean and the drain
free of grease so it
doesn't back up in the
apartment downstairs
or that I don't spill
coffee on the stove
and detonate the
delicate electrical
workings?

Isn't it enough that
I keep the TV tuned
24 hours a day to
the protesters in
Beirut or the ads
for exercise where
naked people take
the glow of roasted
Thanksgiving turkeys?

Isn't it enough that
I make my payments
on time, that I am
never late for work,
that I don't dye my
hair or pretend that
this loneliness isn't
murder in progress,

that trying to live
so the authorities

don't notice is
enough to make the
sun rise red like a
fertilized egg in
a frying pan, its
trace of veins and
arteries leading to
a heart as monstrous
as a baby's fist, a
collecting of dust
on an old lady's
figurines, the turn
of a key to a dark
apartment smelling
of the beast whose
lair is the solemn
articulation of
grief and desire and
pornography?

Isn't it enough that
I keep my quiet, that
I write poems and
then throw them away?
Isn't it enough? Well,
isn't it?

AFFECTION

I want to know the
secret of happiness,
and if possible,
could I know by

Tuesday noon? I've
got a meeting with
an important client
and if I know by
then I'd have the
advantage in the
negotiations.
Moreover, I don't
want a partial
answer like that
provided by sex.
When I was a horny
teenager nobody
told me that I
would have to be
in love or else
go to prostitutes
or become one
myself. You see,
I want something
quick, clean and
easy to prepare.
Something in its
own container so
I can toss it out
without messing up
any pots and pans.
Okay? So tell me
the secret. My visa
and Mastercard
are ready.

MEETINGS WITH A SAINT

All you bring with you is
the talent for alcohol.
But I don't complain. I
like the way your thumb
wipes the sweat from your
glass, the way change
accumulates on the bar,
how you smile so soft and
cruel at the pontificates
caught in the glare of
The Game of the Week. If
it's all you bring, that's
enough because unmotivated
companionship is a rare
commodity, something to be
praised when men made
plastic grin from every
corner of the landscape,
their lips tight, whether
in exertion or rest. No,
you my saint, are someone
to be revered, someone who
has transformed himself into
a hundred mouths and two
hundred ears. I like the
way you soak yourself with
noise and smoke and settle
into the soft cushioning
of alcohol. I like that. I
know I'm not supposed to,
but I do. I really do.

TRANSLATING

We were two boys in bathing
suits hanging by our fingers
from the lip of the apartment
house pool.

He said to me, "Somehow all
that learning has to translate
into numbers." I wondered how
he knew that or was it something
he heard his stepfather say?

I still think of that when I
am waiting in traffic or alone
at a bar waiting for someone
who may or may not show.

I try to envision how things
translate and I fail except
for the image of a seashell,
the sound of the sea trapped
inside even though it rests
on a vanity in a bathroom in
a duplex in Tucson, Arizona.

THE ROAD OF LIFE

The most upsetting
thing was when our
column came under
attack. Two privates
and the sergeant-

major were wounded.
When we loaded them
out of the APC the
sergeant-major was
still alive, but
when the transport
arrived in Kabul
the nurse said,
"Why did you bring
him here? Can't you
see he is already
dead?" I couldn't
explain that at the
time it was the
right thing to do,
that we believed
that things could
get no worse. In
his day, Alexander
the Great passed
this way. He called
it the Road of Life.
I'm certain his
commanders and
drivers thought
he was being cruel.

JEWEL LAKE

It was snowing when we reached Jewel Lake.
It was so cold our shovels made no bite
in the earth. We had tents but no stakes

or poles. We slept like wolves huddled
against the night. In the morning we

marched, the lake always to our left until
we reached the railhead and were separated
into groups of ten. Spring passed, then
summer, and when I feel the cold I remember
my brother. Do his callouses open like mine?

Does he tremble when he smells diesel?
When I hear the train winding through the
pass above Jewel Lake I remember the morning
we were detained. Twenty deep on the platform,
his chin on my shoulder, promising nothing
would happen to me.

ON THE WAY OF VEGAS

"What's the purpose
of getting married?"
she asked.

"I don't know," I said.
"Have kids. Have a
big wedding. Not be
alone when you're
old and sick."

She touched the seek
button trying to
find a station that
played something
other than rock and
roll.

I wanted to say,
"It makes no sense
to worry about it
now." But the inside
of the car suddenly
filled with the
sound of a string
quartet.

"Debussy," she said,
sliding into the
hollow of her seat,
tugging the hem of
her skirt over her
knees before lighting
a cigarette.

"Too late now," I
said. "Maybe," she
said. "Maybe not."

SOUP

What is it to have your wife
take your hands and stare
at them as if they were the
paws of an unclassified beast,

for her to say the word "soup"
as she massages each knuckle,
the cortex of her dreaming
consciousness suddenly vivid,

a mutter of freesias, each
colored pink and amber and

black with the desire she has
not just for you but for all

men, everywhere. And you stare
at your hands, humble and
angry as they are, and they
seek some comfort from the
spoon, from the syllable "soup."

IN KENSINGTON

We were always from the outskirts,
sizing still stiff in our shirts
as we pedaled through the lines of
palm on either side of the street.

In the quiet of the afternoon you
could hear the wind rustle way up
in the leaves. That was on quiet
afternoons. The rest of the time

it was who was who and what was
what. No history. No desire. Our
voices thick in our chests, or so
we thought. It was either then or

now and now is now and at night in
bed we listen to the sound the
sprinklers make on the Republican's
yard. "In New York," you say, but

honey, this ain't Long Island and
what was fine and fair sits in the
driveway, 300 a month, not counting
the insurance.

DOROTEA REYNA

MY FATHER

My father had the most
beautiful voice:
black keys on
white,
under the disdained
crown of a Mexican name

My father took to music—
violent his ways,
my father's days a pattern
of sunflowers & knives

Take a man gold
as the dust
on the sunflower's face,
a man darker even
than her dark face

Take a man more precise
than the sunflower's
sharp blade,
and place him in a cage—

More learned than the sum
on an abacus
of infinite terrain,

More primitive
than hate

My father more learned,
more primitive,
his heart a violent sonnet

VOICE

I.
For a long time
I held
my breath;
the pressure grew
but somehow did not kill.

Thoughts
streamed from my ears
edging towards the water's
surface. Suicides.

Sometimes
the pain was intense:
as if a fish
breathed fire, or sand.

Voice?
I had none.
Imagining that such a gift,
like so many others,
was the providence of them.

A voice,
I dreamed,
was a runaway horse
in a green field.

II.
So I tried to look
like them. Walk and talk
and ride like them.
The black flower
I learned as a girl,
I traded for the lily.

For someone with no
voice, I gave away my own
quickly enough. Black bull,
vernacular, precious native seed.
I gave it away just like that.
Like Malinche, and for
her reasons.

III.
My own voice,
the sounds that came from my
throat, were so many
colored scarves, illusions.
Designed to please, ease
away anger, or charm. Ironically,
to harm. My words, spiked traps.

They came up from me,
these errant sounds, like flowers
exploding, a bludgeoned geometry.

Taken as if by wind
to the four directions, or wherever
they were needed, at whatever time.
Wasted like tissues. Offhand.

The miracle was that
they took me at my word.

Hurling stone balls through stone hoops.
Playing at ritual, theirs.

   IV.
To have a
voice . . .

My own sounds ghosts,
circus mirrors.

I could never manage
that sleight of hand. Could never
take that deep a breath . . .

   V.
A crevice I navigate:
a fierce wound, a wary angel.
A birthday present
with no lid, no bow.
A little bird I have to coax.

Sometimes I sit
in my room and think about voice.
Wondering how to bounce it.
How to catch it. How to sew
it to my skin so it can't stray.

Sometimes language,
sounds, my voice, comes up
to my ears and I feel it
tilting like water
in a cup—

JOEL ANTONIO VILLALÓN

Blue Day

The day was blue, and the young man carrying a briefcase
smiled to the sun. His steps bobbed as shadows of leaves dap-
pled his face, and he wanted to dance, because white buds
had once again appeared on the trees outside his bedroom
window now that the snows had melted. He hated the empty
feeling that winter left in him, and today, that emptiness,
that loneliness, which accompanied winter was gone. Today
felt new to the young man, the air clean and cold, and he
hummed loudly strolling on the street. "What a great day," he
thought. "Spring every year should start on days like today;
bright, brisk, clear days."

The thought of the season changing filled his memory with
a warm surge of images: the penetrating smells of thawing
earth, the bright whites of flowering dogwoods and the resonating sounds of returning robins. A very cold wind grazed
the young man, and he picked up his pace. He shivered and
smiled at his impatience with winter lingering the way it
was, and he stopped and set his briefcase down. As he buttoned his heavy overcoat, he noticed a child on the sidewalk
standing against a red brownstone. "What a tiny thing," the
young man thought. "Should he be here alone?" The tiny
child examined the young man with soulful eyes; his legs
were crossed, his palms seemed stuck to bricks on each side of
him. His coat was well padded and buttoned, and he looked,
to the young man, like a furry, round ball.

"Smnpht . . . tript . . . crt . . . treet," the child mumbled.

The young man walked to the child. "What?" he said.

The child peered at his feet, lifted his arm and pointed, "Mnpt . . . crot treet."

The man straightened and looked up the steps to the brownstone. He saw no one; then turning, he squinted his eyes and scanned the roadway. Cars came from both directions. No one walked on the sidewalks.

"Where are your parents?" he looked down to the child. "Do they know where you are?"

"Mmpt . . . cropt," he whispered.

"I don't understand you. What do you want?" The man looked around again. "Do you want to cross the street? Is that it? Is that what you want?" The child pointed a stubby finger to the corner and mumbled, but the man did not comprehend his sounds. "Do you want to cross?" the young man said louder.

The child slid two steps sideways from the man into the shade of the stoop and looked down.

The man chuckled, shook his head, picked up his briefcase and started off again. He had taken two steps when he heard a scream, "Aaagh!" He swerved, off balance, looking to the street. He then turned and saw the child standing to his side. The child pointed with both hands to the corner and shouted, "Treet . . . preeth!"

"Where are your parents?" the man yelled. "You scared me to death, you know that?"

"Treeth!" the child screamed.

"C'mon, . . . I don't believe this." He took a step toward the child, and the child ran to the shadow of the stoop. "Listen," he shouted, "if you want me to help you, you're gonna have to tell me what you want."

The child took a step back further, "Spreeee!"

The young man stood shaking his head. He could see the child's breath in the shadow, and he turned and noticed a tall man approaching them down the sidewalk.

"What's the matter?" the tall man said as he neared.

"Nothing's the matter," the young man said. "I don't know

who this kid is. I was just standing here . . . " He leaned toward the tall man, "Is he yours?"

"No, he's not," the man replied. "What's the matter? Is
he hurt?"

"Look, I didn't touch him or anything. I don't know who he
is. I was on my way to work, and he was standing here, and
he started talking to me, but I can't understand a word he
says." The young man took a breath, "He may want to cross
the street."

The tall man's eyes remained on him. "Well," he said.

"Well, what?"

"Does he want to cross the street?"

"Oh, I don't know," the young man shrugged, "I don't know
that for sure."

The tall man lowered himself on one knee before the child,
smiled and looked at the child. "Hi, my name's Bob. I live
around the corner. Do you live around here?" The tall man
waited. The child looked at him and said nothing.

"Well . . . let's see, are you waiting for your mommy or
daddy?" The child lowered his head. The tall man glanced up
to the man. He slowly drew closer and gently placed his fingers on the child's shoulder and whispered, "I'm going to cross
the street right now. Would you like to come with me across
the street?"

The child drew a heavy breath.

"This street right here. I'm going to cross this street now.
Would you like to come with me?" The child took another
breath, then meekly nodded.

The tall man looked up again and said, "It's O.K., I'm not
late for work. I'll take care of it."

The young man stood there, not knowing what to say,
and he clumsily raised his briefcase to them and woodenly
started off, but, after a few steps, he felt he should thank the
other man, but he did not know why. He turned to say something, but the tall man and the child were walking from him.
The tall man was saying something to the child the young

man could not hear, moving his head, swinging his briefcase. The child held onto the tall man's free arm and surveyed him quietly. The young man sullenly watched. Shadows from the new leaves fluttered across his face and another cold breeze blew down the street. He lifted the collar of his coat and continued looking at the couple. The sun shone brilliantly on them as they took very small, slow steps. Cars stopped to let them pass, and when they reached the other side, the child let the man go and awkwardly crawled up some stairs and tapped on a door. After a moment, the door creaked open, and the child quickly disappeared through the gap.

About the Contributors

FRANCISCO X. ALARCÓN
is a poet, editor, and critic who writes in both English and Spanish. His most recent publication, *Body in Flames/Cuerpo en llamas*, is a bilingual collection of poems published in 1990. A third-generation Californian, Alarcón spent much of his childhood in Mexico. He currently teaches at the University of California, Santa Cruz.

GLORIA E. ANZALDÚA
is a Chicana *tejana* lesbian-feminist poet and fiction writer, now living in Santa Cruz, California. She is co-editor of *This Bridge Called My Back: Writings by Radical Women of Color* (1983), winner of the Before Columbus Foundation American Book Award. Her book *Borderlands/La frontera: The New Mestiza* (1987) has been highly acclaimed. She is the editor of a recently published collection, *Making Face, Making Soul/ Haciendo Caras: Creative and Critical Perspectives of Women of Color* (1990). She has taught creative writing, Chicano studies, and feminist studies at several universities.

IVAN ARGÜELLES
was raised in Mexico City, Mexicali, Los Angeles, and Rochester, Minnesota, and has authored eleven poetry collections; the latest, *Looking for Mary Lou*, received the 1989 William Carlos Williams Award from the Poetry Society of America. He has published frequently in literary magazines and journals. He is a librarian at the University of California, Berkeley.

ALFREDO ARTEAGA
is an assistant professor of English at the University of California, Berkeley, where he lectures on literary theory, Chicano

literature, and Shakespeare. His poem, "Letters of Color," is from his forthcoming book of poetry, *Cantos*.

ENRIQUE BERUMEN
was born in East Los Angeles but also lived in Tijuana and Mexico City. He received his degree in Creative Writing from the University of California, Santa Cruz, and studied basic film/videomaking at the International School of Cinema in Cuba. Presently, he studies screen writing.

NORMA CANTÚ
received her Ph.D. in English from the University of Nebraska-Lincoln in 1982, and is currently an associate professor of English at Laredo State University. Her research interests include folklore, Chicana writers, and feminist criticism. She has published and lectured on the subjects of *matachines* and Chicanas. She has published poetry in *Huehuetitlán* and *The Prairie Schooner*.

SANDRA CISNEROS
was born in Chicago and is the recipient of two NEA fellowships for poetry and fiction. Cisneros makes her living as a migrant professor. She has taught at California State University at Chico, the University of California at Berkeley and Irvine, the University of Michigan, and the University of New Mexico. When she is not teaching, she likes to live in San Antonio, Texas. Her books include *The House on Mango Street* (Vintage), *My Wicked Wicked Ways* (Third Woman), and *Woman Hollering Creek* (Random House). Daughter of a Mexican father, a Mexican-American mother, and sister to six brothers, she is nobody's mother and nobody's wife.

C. S. FOSTER
was born in California and raised on the U.S.—Mexican border. He lives in Napa, California, and writes poetry because "I can't seem to leave words alone."

ODILIA GALVÁN RODRÍGUEZ

grew up on the south side of Chicago with her mother, two brothers, and sister. In the summers, she lived with relatives who would come north each spring to work the fields. She has been a political activist and writer since age fifteen. Her work has appeared in *Just Thoughts*, *Little Bird*, and *Matrix*. She now lives in Berkeley.

RAMÓN GARCÍA

grew up in the Central Valley of California. He doesn't live there anymore but considers it home. He says that home for him "is where my voice comes from." His work has appeared in *Quarry West 25*, *Chinguapin*, *Revista Mujeres*, and *El Andar*.

ALICIA GASPAR DE ALBA

is the author of a collection of poetry, *Beggar on the Cordoba Bridge*, and of a forthcoming collection of short fiction, *The Mystery of Survival and Other Stories*. She was awarded a Massachusetts Artists Fellowship in Poetry in 1989. She migrated back to Albuquerque where she now lives.

BARBARA RENAUD GONZÁLEZ

grew up in the Texas Panhandle. She chose to attend Pan American University on the *frontera* where she received her B.A. in Social Work in 1974. Her M.S.W. is from the University of Michigan, and she has done postgraduate work at Harvard. She presently lives in Dallas and works as a consultant in community development for the Dallas County Community College District.

RAY GONZÁLEZ

is the author of two books of poetry including *Twilights and Chants*, which was awarded a 1987 Four Corners Book Award. He has edited several anthologies of poetry and has three books forthcoming: *After Aztlán: Latino Poets in the Nine-*

ties, *This Is Not Where We Began: Interviews with Latino Writers*, and *The Texas Poetry Anthology*. He is now Literature Director of the Guadalupe Cultural Arts Center in San Antonio.

CÉSAR A. GONZÁLEZ-T.

is a professor at San Diego Mesa College. His books include his poetry, *Unwinding the Silence* (1987), and his edited collection of essays, *Anaya: Focus on Criticism* (1990). His work recently appeared in *Talking from the Heart: An Anthology of Men's Poetry*. He tells us: "Myth is a secular intuition of infinity within. I believe that beauty 'ever ancient, ever new' abides."

JUAN FELIPE HERRERA

is a playwright and poet with four books of poetry: *Rebozos of Love*, *Exiles of Desire*, *Facegames*, and *Akrilica*. He received the Before Columbus American Book Award for *Facegames*, as well as two NEA fellowships and four California Arts Council Artist awards. He was a Breadloaf Fellow in 1990. His poetry has appeared in many journals in the United States and abroad including *American Poetry Review, Zyzzyva, El gallo ilustrado*, and *Espacio libre*. He holds an M.F.A. in poetry from the Iowa Writers Workshop. He presently lives in Fresno and teaches at California State University, Fresno.

JOEL HUERTA

was born and raised in Edinburg, Texas, in the Lower Rio Grande Valley. He is a graduate of Rice University and the Writing Program at the University of Arizona. He recently completed a manuscript entitled *Las Chrome Doors of Heaven*, and currently lives and works in Tucson.

DARREN J. DE LEÓN

is a student at the University of California, Riverside. His work has appeared in *Nuestra Cosa* (the Chicano newspaper

at UCR), *New Visions of Aztlán, Garden Club Newsletter,*
and *Mosaic.* Darren, who has always referred to himself as a
Chicano, prides himself in "always being ready for the
revolution."

VICTORIANO MARTÍNEZ,

who was born and raised in Fresno, California, now lives in
San Francisco. He is finishing a book of essays on Chicano/
Latino artists and poets for which he received the John Mc-
Carron New Writing in Arts Criticism Grant. He attended
California State University, Fresno, and Stanford University.
He has published poems in several magazines and journals in-
cluding *El Tecolote Literario, Zyzzyva,* and *The Berkeley Po-
etry Review.* His short story, "The Baseball Glove," appeared
in the *The Iowa Review.*

PAT MORA,

a Kellog National Fellow, is the author of two poetry collections, *Chants* and *Borders,* both published by Arte Público
Press. Her children's book, *Tomás and the Library Lady,* was
published in 1991. A native of El Paso, she now lives in
Cincinnati.

RAÚL NIÑO

lives in Chicago where he is a member of Movimiento Artís-
tico Chicano (MARCH). He has been featured on DIAL-
A-POEM in Chicago and published in *Tonatzín* and the anthology, *Emergency Tacos.* His first collection of poetry,
Breathing Light, was published in 1990.

ORLANDO RAMÍREZ

was born in Tucson in 1955. After graduating from Yale University he moved to San Jose, California, where he spent several years working with Mango Publications. In 1979 he won
a first prize for poetry in the University of California, Irvine,
Chicano Literary Contest. He quit writing for nine years only
to begin to practice his craft again two years ago. He pres-

ently lives in San Diego where he works for a major wire service.

DOROTEA REYNA
was born and raised in the Rio Grande Valley of south Texas. She received her B.A. in English from Stanford University and her M.A. in English from the University of Texas at Austin. She writes poetry, short stories, and plays, and presently lives in the Bay Area.

ANDRÉS RODRÍGUEZ
received his M.A. from the Graduate Writing Program at Stanford University and his Ph.D. from the University of California, Santa Cruz. His poems have appeared in *Wilderness*, *Quarry West*, and various little magazines. He presently teaches at the University of Arizona.

LUIS OMAR SALINAS
was born in Robstown, Texas, in 1937. He later moved to California where he attended various colleges. He published his first book of poetry, *Crazy Gypsy*, in 1970. Since 1980, he has published *Afternoon of the Unreal*, *Darkness Under the Trees*, *Walking Behind the Spanish*, *Prelude to Darkness*, *Selected Works*, and *Sadness of Days*. In 1988 he published a chapbook, *The Survivors*. He lives in Sanger, California, where he writes and works as an interpreter.

ELBA SÁNCHEZ
is a Chicana who was born in Mexico and grew up in San Francisco. Poetry and performance have been her focuses. Most recently, she portrayed Frida Kahlo in *When Will I Dance?*, a production of Santa Cruz Actors' Theater. Her work has been published in various anthologies and journals. She is founding co-editor of *Revista Mujeres*. She presently teaches at the University of California, Santa Cruz.

GARY SOTO

is the author of six poetry books and six prose books. His forthcoming works are the young adult novel *Taking Sides*, and *Learning Religion*, both due in 1991. His first film is *The Bike*.

JOEL ANTONIO VILLALÓN

was raised in south Texas, has lived in Boston and New York City, and now lives in San Francisco. Villalón is currently working on a collection of stories and is planning graduate study in creative writing. His work has appeared in *Puerto del Sol*.

HELENA MARÍA VIRAMONTES'

first book, *The Moths and Other Stories*, has been very favorably reviewed and is in its second printing. Viramontes has been invited to lecture and read throughout the Southwest and California as well as in the People's Republic of China. She is currently completing her second collection of short stories, *Paris Rats in L.A.* and a half-hour teleplay for Ana María García, an American Film Institute Awardee.

MARY-ELISE WHEATWIND,

a *coyote* of mixed heritage, is half Chicana, one-quarter Swedish, and one-quarter Russian Jew. She has a B.A. in Creative Writing from San Francisco State University and an M.A. in English from the University of California, Berkeley. Her work has been awarded two California Arts Council Literature Grants, and a PEN Syndicated Fiction Prize. She presently lives in Albuquerque.

BERNICE ZAMORA

currently teaches Chicano and Native American literatures and a course on Third World Women Writers in the United States at Santa Clara University. A book of old and new poems is forthcoming by Bilingual Press. Zamora now lives in Santa Clara, California.